THE UNRAVELLING OF MGNREGA

THE UNRAVELLING OF MGNREGA

A COMPARATIVE STUDY OF BIHAR, CHHATTISGARH, JHARKHAND, MADHYA PRADESH, ODISHA AND UTTAR PRADESH

ARCHANA SINHA
DENZIL FERNANDES

Indian Social Institute

GYAN

Published, 2019

Published by

Gyan Publishing House
5, Ansari Road
Daryaganj, New Delhi-110002
Phone: 011-47034999, 9811692060
www.gyanbooks.com
E-mail: books@gyanbooks.com

and

Indian Social Institute
10, Institutional Area
Lodi Road, New Delhi - 110003
Phone: (011) 49534132/133

Printed at: G. Print Process, Delhi.

Cataloging in Publication Data—DK
Courtesy: D.K. Agencies (P) Ltd. <docinfo@dkagencies.com>

Sinha, Archana, *Dr.*, **author.**
The unravelling of MGNREGA : a comparative study of Bihar, Chhattisgarh, Jharkhand, Madhya Pradesh, Odisha and Uttar Pradesh / Archana Sinha and Denzil Fernandes.
pages cm
Includes bibliographical references.
ISBN 9788189762698

1. India. Mahatma Gandhi National Rural Employment Guarantee Act, 2005. 2. Rural poor—Employment—India. 3. Rural development—Government policy—India. I. Fernandes, Denzil, author. II. Title.

LCC HD5710.85.S56 2019 | DDC 331.110954 23

Contents

Foreword

The Government of India has passed the National Rural Employment Guarantee Act NREGA in September 2005, with a broad national consensus. Thus was hailed as a momentous part of legislation and people's act by several thinkers and writers on Panchayati Raj and Rural Development. The act provides for the enhancement of livelihood security of the households in the rural areas by providing at least one hundred days of guaranteed wage employment in every financial year to every household whose adult members volunteer to do unskilled manual labour.

Nrega is a people's act. Its effective implementation depends on peoples participation and programme implementation. The individual has to be transparent and accountable to the people. NREGA is as a wage employment programme also seeks to create productive assets at the level of the village that serve as common facilities. NREGA has generated considerable enthusiasm among the rural people of our country given its features of statutory time bound provision for providing employment, demand-based approach, shift from being work-led to employment generation, focus on accountability and transparency and compensation (in the form of unemployment allowance) in case of non-provision of employment. It is a matter of great pride that the act has brought about a paradigm shift, both in the design and approach of our earlier intervention mechanisms for wage employment programmes. Thus MGNREGA is implemented in the spirit intended by ensuring transparency and vigilance, people's participation, monitoring, evaluation and public accountability. This book attempts to capture early trends of the programme awareness, implementation, and voices of the people whose lives have been impacted in its initial years of implementation.

This book not only introduces the reader with MGNREGA but also explains the impact of it on rural urban migration and rural livelihood. It describes the challenges and opportunities of MGNREGA towards transforming rural India and empowerment of the poor. Finally the implementation and impact assessment of MGNREGA is studied in some selected districts of states, like Bihar, Chhattisgarh, Odisha, Jharkhand, Madhya Pradesh, and Uttar Pradesh.

Dr. Denzil Fernandes
Executive Director,
Indian Social Institute, New Delhi

Acknowledgements

I acknowledge and express my sincere appreciation and thanks to all those persons who have been associated with the study **"Implementation Status and Impact of MGNREGA in Bihar, Chhattisgarh, Jharkhand, Madhya Pradesh, Odisha and Uttar Pradesh"** and have helped to bring it to completion. My sincere thanks to Dr. Denzil Fernandes (Executive Director, Indian Social Institute, New Delhi), Dr. Joe Xavier (Former Executive Director, Indian Social Institute, New Delhi) and Dr. John Chathanatt (Former Research Director, Indian Social Institute, New Delhi) for their continuous support and guidance to bring the study to completion.

I acknowledge the support and help rendered from field based organizations and agencies in Bihar, Chhattisgarh, Jharkhand, Madhya Pradesh, Odisha and Uttar Pradesh, which extended their support, for their help in coordinating the data collection work through their dedicated team members. I am thankful to all those beneficiaries' and non-beneficiaries' respondents from the field for giving their precious time during filling up questionnaires in the field. They deserve my thanks for their active participation and help in initiating the field investigation and data collection from the field as research staff of project team.

I further extend my thanks to the faculty and staff members at Indian Social Institute, New Delhi for their cooperation all through. My special thanks to library staff for their patient help in carrying out the project. My thanks to Ms Nazia Ansari, Ms. Samreen, and Ms. Satyabhama from Indian Social Institute for their patient help in typing work and data entry work into SPSS software. I must acknowledge various field level agencies, government departments, institutions and websites for providing data and information to carry out the project successfully.

Dr. Archana Sinha
Department of Women's Studies,
Indian Social Institute, New Delhi

Glossary of Abbreviations

APO	-	Assistant Programme Officer
BDO	-	Block Development Officers
BPL	-	Below Poverty Line
CAG	-	Comptroller and Auditor General
CEFS	-	Centre for Environment and Food Security
CPIAL	-	Consumer Price Index for Agricultural Labour
CSE	-	Centre for Science and Environment
DPC	-	District Programme Coordinator
DPRD	-	Department of Panchayat and Rural Development
DRDA	-	District Rural Development Agent
GBPISS	-	Govind Bhallab Pant Institute of Social Sciences
GP	-	Gram Panchayat
GRS	-	Gram Rojgar Sahayak / Sewak
IAMR	-	Institute of Applied Manpower Research
ISWSD	-	Indian School of Women's Studies Department
JCB	-	JC Bamford Excavators
KBK	-	Kalhandi Bolangir Koraput
LWE	-	Left Wing Extremism
MGNREGS	-	Mahatma Gandhi National Rural Employment Guarantee Scheme
MoRD	-	Ministry of Rural Development
NFIW	-	National Federation of Indian Women
NREGA	-	National Rural Employment Guarantee Act

NREP	-	National Rural Employment Programme
NSS	-	National Sample Survey
OBCs	-	Other Backward Castes
PD	-	Project Director
PEO	-	Panchyat Executive Officer or Panchyat Secretary
PRIA	-	Participatory Research in Asia
PS	-	Panchayat Sevaks
SC	-	Scheduled Caste
SoR	-	Schedule of Rates
SPSS	-	Statistical Package of Social Sciences
SRRA	-	Society for Regional Research and Analysis
ST	-	Scheduled Tribe
TOI	-	Times of India
UPA	-	United Progressive Alliance
WPR	-	Worker Participation Rate

Executive Summary

The passage of the Mahatma Gandhi National Rural Employment Guarantee Act has seen the culmination of vital deliberations on the merits and demerits of the wage employment guarantee programme as an appropriate mechanism for social security and poverty reduction in India. For those populace of India who have negligible economic assets and for farmers who are landless or with small landholdings, MGNREGS has given a new hope. This is a positive and welcome development. This hope can be further strengthened by creating awareness about the scheme and ensuring its effective implementation. The scheme needs to be transformed from being just a means of short-term job provider to long-term sustainable livelihood enhancement initiatives. In the light of this study many insights could be derived and further proposals be given. Sustainable livelihood, employment security, equality, social justice and sustainable rural development in India have assumed greater space in the national community. Sustainable livelihood is the vision of a localized system of self-managing communities and is the balanced interaction among humans, natural resources, technology and environment in favour of human development (Rajhbhandari, 2006). Such insights need to be taken seriously. The sustainable livelihood approach is the people-centred approach as it focuses on empowering local communities, encouraging community consciousness and relationships, and decentralizing social, economic and political powers to women and marginalized groups in particular. Hence, adequate institutional frameworks are required in the area of rural development, and must be initiated with the encouragement of the local leadership and mobilization of the poor (Ghate, 1984).

This primary field-level research study in the states of Bihar, Chhattisgarh, Jharkhand, Madhya Pradesh, Odisha, and Uttar Pradesh reveals that MGNREGS has some extent succeeded in providing employment security to the rural people (39 per cent) during lean season and scarcity of employment opportunities. It is also found that the most vulnerable sections (landless labourers (42 per cent), Scheduled Castes and Scheduled Tribes) are not getting their due share in the MGNREGS. Though, MGNREGS has been giving employment security to the rural poor, its performance is not up to the mark in providing 100-days, employment to each deprived and needy households. It is found that MGNREGS is able to cater to only 32 per cent in providing assured income, a very small percentage of people received at least 100 days of wage employment for which members of a household are available for work. Further, this proportion is very low for most vulnerable, *i. e.,* landless labourers, Scheduled Caste (SC) and Scheduled Tribe (ST) categories. The MGNREGS has partially arrested unemployment, agricultural productivity, women's participation, poverty and out-migration among labourers from these rural areas, as they are now able to make both ends meet within their village during the MGNREGS implementation. Demand driven approach of the MGNREGS is not fully utilized by the rural poor as very few beneficiaries applied for job through proper channel. Several lacunae have been identified in relation to the institutional aspect in implementation of MGNREGS in the selected states. For effective implementation it is advisable to appoint an 'employment guarantee assistant', in each Gram Panchayat called 'Gram Rozgar Sevak', in the local language for this purpose. However, at the Panchayat level, the post of Gram Rojgar Sahayak (GRS) has remained almost vacant in Bihar and Madhya Pradesh. All the works under the scheme was being managed by the Gram Panchayat, who are overburdened with work. Under MGNREGS, the Gram Panchayat is the most important agency for executing MGNREGS works. The MGNREGS envisages that at least fifty percent of the works in terms of cost can be executed by Gram Panchayat.

This continued vulnerability points to the need to adapt and strengthen the transparency safeguards related to wage payments. In the end, the best protection against misappropriation is the empowerment of MGNREGA workers.

Chapter - I

Introduction

India continues to face the paradox of some backward states in the north and eastern regions of the country with dismal poverty while some progressive states in west and southern regions record vibrant growth. Recently a number of backward states like Chhattisgarh, Uttar Pradesh, Jharkhand, Madhya Pradesh, Bihar and Odisha became center of attention for issues such as poverty and unstable growth. The diverse growth poverty-disparity scenario has been pronounced at sub-national level, it has also been reflected in terms of uneven human development, persistent gender inequalities, inter-state and intra-state poverty disparities and fluctuating growth. Hence, the issue of growth and poverty nexus has re-emerged as one of the key policy debates and concerns among the policy makers, social activists, leaders, development planners and researchers. In order to accomplish twin objectives of growth and equity that translate growth into faster poverty reduction and human development focus has been on inclusive growth through development intervention policy and programmes.

The goal of democracy is to endorse freedom, rights and equality to create an egalitarian social order. However, in spite of having a democratic institutional arrangement, with vibrant and practicing democratic norms and constitutional framework, the Indian state could not deliver the desired results for inclusive growth and equitable and sustainable development as envisioned in the Constitution.

The MGNREGA Scheme is directly focused on the rural poor. The condition of the rural poor of India has remained unchanged in spite of the developmental programs planned and promulgated through various five year plans. Over 70 per cent of India's population is rural. Rural poverty accounts for nearly 63 per cent of poverty worldwide (Rural Poverty in Developing Countries: Implications for Public Policy. Mahmood Hasan (http://www.imf.org/external/pubs/ft/issues/issues26/index.htm). In order to reduce, if not eliminate, poverty in India, rural poverty in particular, both the Central and State governments had initiative various projects and programs, especially oriented to employment creation. The National Rural Employment Program 1983-99, Jawahar Rojgar Yojana 1989-1990, Employment Assurance Scheme 1993-1999, Sampoorna Grameen Rojgar Yojna 2001, National food for Work Program 2004 are some of such programs.

The Mahatma Gandhi National Rural Employment Guarantee Scheme (MGNREGS) is a flagship employment guarantee scheme, enacted by legislation on August 25, 2005by government of India under United Progressive Alliance (UPA) government. The act was passed on September 5th and came into force from February 2, 2006 in 200 economically backward districts. It was expanded to cover another 130 districts in 2007-08 and eventually covered all 593 districts in India and 4,49,40,870 rural households were said to have provided jobs under MGNREGS during 2008-09, with an national average of 48 working days per household in April 1, 2008. It was renamed as the Mahatma Gandhi National Rural Employment Guarantee Scheme (MGNREGS) on October 2, 2009. "NREGA has been aptly named after the Father of the Nation as he had always held the concept of Gram Swaraj in high esteem," said the Prime Minister (PM) during a celebration on the 50 years of Panchayati Raj in India. The MGNREGA is a unique act which recognizes the legitimate role of panchayats in addressing their fundamental duty as expressed in the 73rd Constitutional Amendment of providing "economic development and social justice" in their areas. The scheme plans to provide a legal guarantee for one hundred days of employment in every financial year to adult members of any rural household willing to do public work-related unskilled manual work at the statutory minimum wage of Rs.100 per day.

Mahatma Gandhi National Rural Employment Guarantee Act (MGNREGA) is intended to give a legal guarantee of employment to anyone who is willing to do casual manual labor at the statutory minimum wage. Any adult who applies for work under NREGA is entitled to employment in public works within 15 days; otherwise, it is a state responsibility to provide them unemployment benefit. However, this entitlement is subject to some important limitations. For instance, the work guarantee applies in rural areas only, and it is limited to 100 days per household per year. The MGNREGA is based on the principle of self-selection, and it is a step towards legal enforcement of the right to work, as an aspect of the fundamental right to live with dignity. The NREGA also mandates 33 percent participation for women.

The main objective of MGNREGS is rural development and creating employment in rural areas. This act was introduced with an aim of improving the purchasing power of the rural people, primarily of semi or un-skilled workers living in rural India. The MGNREGA stipulates that works must be targeted towards a set of specific rural development activities, such as water conservation and harvesting, afforestation, rural connectivity, flood control, construction and repair of embankments. Digging of new tanks/ponds, percolation tanks, and construction of small check dams are also given importance. The employed are given work in such areas as land leveling, tree plantation, mud digging and so on.

For most of the world, MGNREGS has been a unique phenomenon. It has a demand-driven design, rights-based structure and unprecedented scale of investment by the Union government. Many scholars, researchers, social activists, policy makers and analysts around the world have intensely studied its implementation. Several studies have shown that works under MGNREGS have been fruitful in providing livelihood and income security, increased food intake, decreased incidence of poverty and improved health outcomes. Bela Bhatia and Jean Drèze (2002)[1], based on their experience in Manika and Manatu in Latehar district, Jharkhand, assert that MGNREGS has become a matter of great interest in the rural areas, that there is growing awareness of the promise of "100 days of employment for every household" and widespread demand for job cards. Government officials such as Block Development Officers (BDO) and Panchayat Sevaks (PS) find themselves compelled to devote a considerable part of their work time to MGNREGS-related matters, due not only to orders from the top but also to rising pressures from below.

The states have launched new schemes to be fed by lavish NREGA funds. These schemes, bearing the names of states, pertain to works allowed under the job scheme like digging ponds, making roads and constructing water tanks. The trend is widespread. Madhya Pradesh has launched Kapil Dhara scheme for ponds in locations where there are SC/ST population, 'Nirmal Neer' and 'baramasi sadak yojana'; Uttar Pradesh has 'adarsh talab yojana'; and Rajasthan has 'harit Rajasthan' and 'keshav vadi yojana'. Chhattisgarh has a small scheme too. They are called 'sub-schemes' under NREGA. Local names are being given to projects and schemes under MGNREGA which is not permissible. The only caption which can be given to works under job scheme is MGNREGA. The institution of sub-schemes devised by states threatens to push MGNREGA to the background while using its funds. To many, it is a new attempt by states to appropriate the politically beneficial scheme. It is, in fact, an improvement on their earlier method of prefixing the state's name to NREGA. It was renamed by prefixing 'MG' to the name to stop the trend (TOI, 2010).[2]

Geographical Area

The study will be undertaken in the states of Uttar Pradesh, Madhya Pradesh, and Chhattisgarh, Jharkhand, Odisha, and Bihar. These states are among the poor states in central India. The implementation status of MGNREGS in some pockets of these states remain very poor as comparatively with several other Indian states in areas like - person-days of MGNREGS, employment per rural household, share of women in MGNREGS employment, share of wages in total expenditure, and average wage cost per person-day as reported in several research reports.

More than seventy one per cent of Indian labour force and more than 70 per cent of Indian population lives in rural India. They not only live in rural areas but majority of them (56.5 percent of the total workers) earn their livelihood from agriculture. This shows a low level of diversification of occupation in the rural areas. The distressed rural economy has triggered large scale migration from rural to urban areas, as well as intra and inter-state migration. In this background, we are trying to understand rural poverty in the selected six states and how MGNREGS is changing, if at all, the rural face.

- **Bihar**

The rural livelihood, sustainable development, environmental problems and jobless growth are concerns of Bihar today. However the actual condition in terms of trends in economic growth in Bihar seems to be far from this. In this context of changed political scenario and overall improving economic growth, this study may be an initiative that reflects on policy and academic debate on contemporary Bihar vis-à-vis development process in rural India. The MGNREGS in Bihar, as in many other states, has been quite controversial in both the policy as well as implementation, as observed by research communities. Its implementation and impact are under study by various researchers and policy think tanks. Directly pertinent to our analysis are awareness, process of implementation and impact of the project on rural Bihar. The study also makes its observation on MGNREGS works too often allocated on the basis of social status, personal connections, or corruption; thereby undercutting MGNREGS's self-targeting design and its capacity to reduce poverty. Therefore, this study on Bihar looks for mapping the implementation and impact of MGNREGA both horizontally looking into the inter-district and intra-district comparisons and vertically MGNREGA's impact on social and political profile of rural Bihar in terms of caste, class and gender.

- **Chhattisgarh**

Chhattisgarh is located in central India. It is one among the few landlocked states in the country. It shares borders with the states of Madhya Pradesh and Maharashtra in the West, Uttar Pradesh and Bihar in the North, Odisha in the East and Andhra Pradesh in the South. As per 2011 census, Chhattisgarh has a population of 22.59 percent. If the trend continues, there would be pressure on the state to provide the basic minimum services to its population. However, the state has a very low population density - 189 persons per sq.km in Chhattisgarh compared to 382 persons per sq. km for all India. Chhattisgarh is one of the sparsely populated with very remote and difficult to reach terrain with almost 44 per cent of its land covered with dense forests. 12.19 per cent of the total population of Chhattisgarh belongs to the Scheduled Castes of which 82.30 per cent belong to rural areas and rest (17.70 per cent) to the urban areas *(http://cg.nic.in/cgbsap/summary.PDF)*. There are 42 tribal groups which are further divided into their sub groups / castes. The primary sector employs a major part of the population, with agriculture being the mainstay of the people. The worker participation of females is very low in Chhattisgarh. The Worker Participation Rate (WPR) in Chhattisgarh was 47.7 percent, 54.3 percent for males and 41 percent for females. The southern and eastern districts have the highest worker participation rates, all well above fifty percent. Chhattisgarh has shown a decade population growth rate of 18.06 per cent. Lacks of adequate transport network, remote villages and dense forest cover have been deterrents to the government's efforts in delivering services to people.

MoRD (2010)[3], in its 'report to people' on MGNREGS describes convergence of different program and establishing synergy between them by the government of Chhattisgarh. Report concluded that Chhattisgarh has under taken convergence initiatives for optimizing the irrigation capacity of all the major, medium and minor projects. The district administration has weaved together the objectives of employment guarantee and overall objectives of the development schemes under state plan/non-plan and central plan in these sectors. Hence, Chhattisgarh was selected for the study in order to understand the implementation status and its impact to make the scheme more effective for the rural poor.

• Jharkhand

In Jharkhand, nearly 28 per cent population belong to the (Scheduled Tribes) ST and 12 per cent to the SC (Scheduled Caste) categories. The state has a population density of 274 persons per sq. km. Jharkhand is a poor state, with per capita income of Rs. 4,161 per annum. All its 24 districts are covered by MGNREGS. When NREGS commenced, Jharkhand had 22 districts; 20 of these were initially covered. The remaining two districts were added under coverage in the second phase of the programme. In the third phase, the two newly formed districts of Khunti and Ramgarh were added. Meanwhile, Jharkhand has been criticized by the central government for poor implementation of the scheme. The utilisation capacity of the state for these schemes is set to be enhanced mainly because the state now has elected rural bodies to plan and execute development in their respective command area. There are about 32,000 revenue villages in the state. After the Panchayati Raj (India) (PRI) elections, as many as 4500 elected panchayats have been constituted across the state. Unfortunately, the tremendous potential of MGNREGS is being wasted due to massive corruption and difficulties in implementation. The corruption is an outcome of the strong nexus between government officials, contractors and middlemen. Transparency safeguards are routinely violated and the funds are being siphoned off. To ensure transparency through the involvement of the community at the planning and monitoring stages, the principal role in the scheme is entrusted to Gram Panchayats. Coupled with the Right to Information Act, this legislation is seen as a harbinger of a silent revolution in the rural areas of Jharkhand in particular.

• Odisha

Odisha has been one of the poorest states in India. Among the 15 major states, Odisha ranked 14th in regards to the living conditions of its people (Behera and Mitra, 1998)[4]. Despite being endowed with rich mineral deposits, forest, fertile land, and plentiful resources, 46.8 per cent of its people live below the poverty line as against the all India average of 28.3 per cent (Planning Commission 2004-05 based on MRP consumption)[5]. Despite various economic development plans and at the plethora of poverty eradication schemes in the state, available data and the studies done in this context have shown that the situations have remained unchanged.

Thus, poverty is an overwhelmingly rural phenomenon in Odisha and closely related to lack of work available, low wages, dependency on small and marginal farming and faulty implementation of government social security schemes. As a result it is seen that every year thousands of rural poor along with their families migrating out in the condition of distress in search of an employment opportunity. According to the estimation of Migration Information and Resource Centre, Odisha, out of 30 million seasonal migrant laborers, Odisha share 2.5 million and is considered as one of the key states to supply migrant laborers. In addition, the center also estimated that the western districts of Balangir, Nuapada and Kalahandi are highly prone for the distress migration, which is all migratory movements that are made in conditions where the individual or the household perceive that the only viable livelihood option for moving out of poverty is to migrate. Such distress situation is usually associated with lack of livelihood options, given the limited economic and employment opportunities, as well as drought, crop failure and food insecurity (FAO, 2016b:1) Their estimation from the Balangir district in the year of 2009 shows that the district alone has 1.5 lakh out of 13 lakh people migrated to other states.

Regardless of the developmental programs of the past decades, the living condition of rural poor has remained unchanged and the rural labourers are considered as the most marginalized section of the society (Gupta, 2009). Odisha is one of the Indian states where maximum masses reside in rural areas (62.87 lakh) (Panchayati Raj, Odisha 1997). And out of them 66.37 per cent of families are living below the poverty line (ibid). Prevailing poverty of Odisha leads to multidimensional factors of socioeconomic and political problems including unemployment, underemployment, low wage rate, low income etc. In order to overcome these serious problems, the government of India promulgated the flagship program of National Rural Employment Guarantees act on 7th September, 2005 by ensuring livelihood security to rural unemployment. This is so far considered as the biggest poverty alleviation program in the world. In the context of Odisha, MGNREG Act came into operation in 19 economically backward districts from 2nd February 2006. It was rolled out in 5 more districts from 1st April 2007 and rest 6 districts were covered under the Act since 1st April 08. Now all 30 districts of Odisha are covered under MGNREGA. Under this backdrop the present study would look into the implementation status and impact of MGNREGA on rural livelihood in four tribal districts of Odisha.

- **Madhya Pradesh**

Bundelkhand is characterised as one of the most backward regions of India comprising of 7 districts of southern Uttar Pradesh, namely Jhansi, Lalitpur, Jalaun, Hamirpur, Mahoba, Banda and Chitrakoot, and 6 districts of northern Madhya Pradesh- Datia, Tikamgarh, Chhatarpur, Panna, Sagar and Damoh. It is a hot and semi-humid region with problem of poor groundwater recharge aggravated by the substratum of impermeable rock. The region falls under the category of ***'drought prone area.'*** Economy of the region is dependent on agriculture and the main source of livelihood is agriculture and related activities. 75 per cent of the people in Bundelkhand depend on agriculture and more than 80 per cent of them are small and marginal farmers. Again 75 percent of the total agriculture is rain-fed. Madhya Pradesh has 39 per cent of its rural population living below the poverty line. MGNREGS has been launched in the state with great hopes, to enhance livelihood security in rural areas by providing at least 100 days of guaranteed wage employment. But the scheme could not achieve its desired goal. According to official statistics, in Madhya Pradesh 96 per cent of the households, who demanded employment, has received employment as against 99 per cent at National level. Less than 20 per cent households received 100 days of employment in last three years. Further, less than 75 per cent sanctioned funds under the scheme could be utilised by the state. Different reports and studies suggest that the pace of the scheme is quite tardy in MP. As stated above Bundelkhand is the most backward region of the state, which needs scheme like MGNREGS for the survival Of The Poorest Section Of The Region.

- **Uttar Pradesh**

Uttar Pradesh has a population of 16.49 percent as per 2011 census. Its share in total area of the country is 7.3 per cent, while its share in country's population is 16.2 per cent *(http://planning.up.nic.in/apd/hdr-2006/chapter-1.pdf)*. Nearly 80 per cent population of U.P. resides in rural area. The high proportion of the population belonging to the socially and economically depressed sections has profound implications for the policy and the status of human development in the state. Economically Uttar Pradesh is among the most backward states of India with high percentage of marginal and small land holdings, high population pressure, and glaring regional imbalances. One of the reasons for the relatively slow economic growth in U.P. is the low level of plan expenditure in the state as compared to the national average and that of the more developed states. Low plan investments in U.P. have been due to the fact that being a poor state it is not able to generate public savings on the required scale. Plan assistance received by U.P. from the centre has also been relatively low especially in the earlier plans.

Motivation For Research

The MGNREGS intends to enhance employment and income for the rural poor and to have the assurance of a basic income for a rather decent survival. How effective is this direct transfer mechanism in reducing poverty in India and particularly in those states which need affirmative action? In order to explore social security through job guarantee and, keeping in view the importance of this act, Indian Social Institute, New Delhi, initiated a research project to map the level of awareness, the implementation status and impact of MGNREGS in six states of India, namely Chhattisgarh, Uttar Pradesh, Jharkhand, Madhya Pradesh, Odisha and Bihar.

The idea of implementation of MGNREGS is premised on the common belief that a legislation is needed to bring about economic development and ushering of social justice which in turn is capable of transforming the rural living condition, increasing sustainable agrarian activities and wholesome economic support of the rural people. Therefore, it is very important to ensure that the scheme is performing well as it ought to be. India is one of the foremost countries where good policies are formulated but they almost utterly fail when implemented at the grassroots. As a result, people are not benefiting from government policies and programs. Hence, Indian Social Institute, being a premier organization working for the right of the marginalized section of the society, proposes to undertake a study on the implementation and impact assessment of MGNREGA with such perspectives. The following are the major objectives of the study.

Objectives

i. To investigate the level of understanding and awareness level about MGNREGS among the villagers at the district level in the state of Chhattisgarh.
ii. To investigate the level of understanding and awareness level about MGNREGS among the government officials and workers at the district level in the state of Chhattisgarh.
iii. To review the current status of the implementation of MGNREGS in the selected state.
iv. To analyse the system and processes emerged during the initiation and execution of the MGNREGS in this state.
v. To study the role of panchayats in the implementation of MGNREGS.
vi. To assess the impact of MGNREGS in the selected panchayats, particularly on economic conditions, livelihood conditions, work availability, degree of participation of the poor and under-privileged section, female empowerment through work participation, and creation of durable rural assets.

vii. To identify emerging strengths and weakness for wider dialogue for improvements.

viii. To suggest measures for effective implementation of the scheme.

This research report looks at the above mentioned objectives of MGNREGS through both qualitative and quantitative parameters of the scheme, keeping in view the larger issues of rural development and poverty mitigation. This research tries to explore the level of awareness, ways of implementation and impact of the scheme by looking onto the following:

- **Awareness Level**

Since it is one of the most progressive acts introduced by the Indian government, the study explores into the level of awareness among villagers about the scheme.

- **Implementation Status**

How MGNREGA has been implemented in the selected states of India and how it is changing the life of rural people. In other words, to review and assess the status of its implementation in these six states.

- **Impact**

In terms of human resources, state machinery involvement and financial outlays it is one of the social security programmes introduced as a flagship programme for rural wellness. Does it secure income and generate capabilities to reduce poverty? In other words, it attempts to study the impact of MGNREGS on the socio-economic condition of rural people in the selected six states. Another objective, as part of the impact analysis through case studies, is to find out how, if any, it is changing the dynamics of socio-political relations at the village level, as awareness and assertiveness of rights under the act disseminate.

This research project on mapping the awareness, implementation status and impact of MGNREGA in the selected six states, interrogates the proposition whether the development model of the Indian state is making village life more egalitarian and independent under the umbrella of MGNREG Scheme. There are various key issues related to conceptualization and contribution of MGNREGS, which this research deals with. In this regard, the study explores the degree to which MGNREGS is effectively helping the rural poor in lifting their livelihood pattern.

Hypothesis

The MGNREGS (the Mahatma Gandhi National Rural Employment

Guarantee Scheme) is no doubt significant for various reasons. It is identified or claimed to be one of the best programmes in the world to provide alternative source of livelihood which will have an impact on reducing migration, growth in education and health care spending and increasing food consumption. Based on the above assumption the study will test the following hypothesis at the field level.

The implementation of the scheme should bring about a positive impact on the socio-economic life of the rural poor. Consequently, there should be fewer instances of hunger, neglect in health care, education and of distress migration.

Inclusion Criteria

Key Respondents

Understanding that MGNREGA is a rural concept, and any inhabitants above 18 years of age irrespective of his/her economic groups are entitled to apply and work under the Act. Therefore, the study considered the households in the villages, no matter whether they are having or not having the job cards, as unit of investigation.

Officials

Considered to those officials who are responsible for the implementation of MGNREGA from the three tier systems i.e the Panchayat, the Block and the District.

Selection Criteria

The study was carried out in **six states** i.e Uttar Pradesh, Madhya Pradesh, Odisha, Bihar, Jharkhand and Chhattisgarh in India on the basis of the marginalization of rural people in terms of poverty, under wage, unemployment and underemployment etc.

A multi stage method was adopted in each state for the selection of the Districts and Blocks and Panchayats. Following the census data (2001), the ST and SC population in each district had been combined and then the top 10 districts with the highest number of combined ST and SC population has been taken. Out of those 10 selected districts, 4 districts on the basis of highest number of rural population have been taken as sample districts.

There are five **Blocks** with the highest number of ST and SC population was selected and then out of 5 selected Blocks, two with highest number of total population was taken for the study. From each Block, two **Panchayat** with highest number of population were selected for the study.

Towards the selection criteria of village, **two villages** from each Panchayat were selected on the basis of highest number of ST and SC population. If in selected Panchayat, there were only **Revenue villages**, then one village was considered for the study. Following the random sampling method the households were selected on the basis of sequence of houses in the village.

Sampling Strategy and Sample Size: Both Purposive and Random sampling were employed to meet the objectives of the study. Understanding that the MGNREGA is applicable for the rural masses and mostly the STs and SCs inhabit in the rural hinterlands. Therefore, the selection of the Districts, the Blocks, and the Panchayats were done **purposively** following the population criterion of STs and SCs and rural population.

In the process 4districts in each state (6 statesx4 districts= 24 districts) and two blocks from each districts (24 districtsx2 blocks= 48 blocks) and two Panchayat in each Block (48 blocks x 2 Panchayat = 96 Panchayat) had been chosen **purposively**. Further, a number of 30 households from each Panchayat were taken **randomly** (either from one or two villages from each Panchayat) (30 household x 96 Panchayat = 2800 households)

Table 1: Sample Details Of Bihar

Name of Districts	*Name of Blocks*	*Name of Panchayat*	*Sample size*
Gaya	Bodhgaya	Mocharim	30
		Khurwama	30
	Fatepur	Bhemo	30
		Turiamba	30
Muzaffarpur	Kudani	Sumara	30
		Fakuli	30
	Mushari	Bhagwanpur	30
		Badajagannath	30
Samastipur	Samastipur	Jitawarpur Nixamat	30
		Punas	30
	Bibhutipur	Desri Karakh	29
		Bibhutipur North	30
Motihari	Kalyanpuri	Parsuniwazid	31
		Kalyanpur	30
	Motihari	Barwa	30
		Ramsingh Chattuni	30

Table 2: Sample Details Of Chhattishgarh

Name of Districts	*Name of Blocks*	*Name of Panchayats*	*Sample Size*
Sareguja	Ambikapur	Nawagarh	**30**
		Khairwar	**30**
	Surajpur	Govindpur	**30**
		Shivandapur	**30**
Raipur	Arang	Nardaha	**30**
		Gullu	**30**
	Dharsinva	Mandhar	**30**
		Kurud Siliyar	**30**
Durg	Paatan	Selud	**30**
		Pahanda	**30**
	Dharmjaygarh	Vijaynagar	**60**
Raigarh	Dharamjaygarh	Sisringa	**60**
	Sarangarh	Godiyari	**30**
		Kosirr	**30**

Table 3: Sample Details Of Jharkhand

Name of Districts	*Name of Blocks*	*Name of thePanchayats*	*Sample size*
Ranchi	Kanke	Boreya	30
		Urgutu	30
	Bero	Khukh	30
		Nahalu/Khapariya	30
Gumla	Sisai	Bondo	30
		Bhargaon	30
	Bherno	Bherno	30
Girdih	Girdih	Fulchi	30
		Jaspur	30
	Deori	Marudih	30
		Asko	30
Ramgarh	Msandu	Mandudih	30
		Manduchati	30
	Patratu	Kurse	30
		Hsariharpur	30

Table 4: Sample Details Of Madhya Pradesh

Name of districts	*Name of Blocks*	*Name of the Gram Panchayat*	*Sample size*
Dhar	Bandwar	Kod	30
		Multan	30
	Sardarpur	Amghera	30
		Desai	30
Sidhi	Shidhi	Padari	30
		Upni	30
	Shidhwal	Vitholi	30
		Amliya	30
Sagar	Sagar	Bithara	30
		Surkhi	30
	Rehali	Gunjara	30
		Patna Bajarg	30
Chindwara	Jamai	Rampur	30
		Datlawadi	30
	Parasia	Umreth	30
		Ravanwada	30

Table 5: Sample Details Of Odisha

Name of Districts	*Name of Blocks*	*Name of the Gram Panchayat*	*Sample size*
Koraput	Boriguma	Boriguma	30
		Sosahandi	30
	Pottangi	Chandaka	30
		Peturu	30
Keonjhar	Baaandspal	Talakadakala	30
		Bayakumutia	30
	Harichandanpur	Pithagola	30
		Sunapentha	30
Mayurbhanj	Badasahi	Pratapur	30
		Durgapur	30
	Kaptipda	Kaptipada	30
		Jayantipatta Samil Jamdiha	30
Sundargarh	Nuagaon	Chitapedi	30
		Nuagaon	30
	Kuarmunda	Kuarmunda	30
		Kumjharia	30

Table 6: Sample Details Of Uttar Pradesh

Name of districts	*Name of Blocks*	*Name of the Panchayats*	*Sample size*
Hardoi	Ahirori	Belapur	60
	Sursa	Surjva	60
Sitapur	Biswara	Kammara Khurd	60
	Godhlamu	Kunara	60
Azamgarh	Thekma	Sarimoha	60
	Bilaraganj	Jolhabegumr	60
Allhabad	Kaudihar	Bamrani Uporhara	60
	Koraun	Belhar	60

Research Methods And Data Collection Tools

Both qualitative and quantitative methods were employed to meet the objectives.

- A combination of open ended and structured and coded Interview schedule was used at household level as well as for the officials included from Panchyat, Block and District level.
- Discussions carried out with implementing officials and the key functionaries/ stake holders and with the villagers at the field level.
- Case study method was employed to capture the real life stories of the beneficiaries in terms of implementation status and its impact in different socio economic life of rural people.

Training of Surveyors

For bringing a common understanding of the objectives, issues relating to MGNREGA and to discuss the questionnaire in brief, and training programmes were organized for the field investigators in each state before the commencement of the data collection.

Pilot Study

A pilot survey was held in the six states to understand the trend of responses. On the basis of findings the questionnaire were eventually modified to incorporate the field leanings.

Data Compilation And Analysis

After the collection of data following the interview schedule, interview guide and through focus group discussion, under the guidance of the research coordinator data were entered in SPSS data analysing format and in Microsoft excel sheet for analysis.

Limitation of The Study

- In many states, it was difficult to find out the Panchayat level data from the census web- site. Hence, before commencing the field study a personal visit was held to collect the Panchyat level data from the District Collectorates and the Block level offices and the process was time consuming.
- Following the 2001 census, the district selections were held, but during the field work it was found that due to the changes in administrative structure the districts were further divided into many more districts. For instance, in the state of Chhattisgarh, following the 2001 census data two districts namely Sarguja and Raipur were selected, but during the field work these two districts were further divided into six districts. Hence a drastic variation was found in terms of ST and SCs population. In those cases the districts were taken as undivided.
- Many of the selected panchayats were converted into municipal bodies. So these municipal bodies had to be skipped during the field work and again following the fixed criteria the next new panchayats were selected for the study.

Panchayat level:

- Gram Rozgar Sewak (GRS)
- Panchyat Executive Officer or Panchyat Secretary
- Sarpanch and ex-sarpanch

Block level:

- Block Development Officer (BDO)
- Assistant Programme Officer (APO)

District level:

- District Collector or Project Director (PD), District Rural Development Agent (DRDA) has been interviewed

Notes

1. B. Bhatia& J. Drèze.(2006). "Employment Guarantee in Jharkand: Ground Realities." Economic and Political Weekly, 41 (29): 3198–3202.
2. The Times of India (7 July 2010).
3. Mahatma Gandhi National Rural Employment Guarantee Act 2005,Report to the People 2nd Feb 2006 to 2nd Feb 2010, Ministry of Rural Development Government of India. New Delhi.
4. Behera, M & A.K Mitra (1998). "The standard of living in India:An attempt towards inter Regional Study", Indian journal of Regional Science, Vol xxxviii, No 2.
5. Retrieved from http://planningcommission.nic.in/news/prmar07.pdf on 3.2.2013.

Chapter - II

Profile of Respondents

This study was designed to know the implementation status and impact of MGNREGA in each of the 6 States, namely Bihar, Chhattisgarh, Jharkhand, Madhya Pradesh, Odisha and Uttar Pradesh. Primary data from each State was collected with a sample of 480 households from four selected districts. Therefore, the overall sample from all the six states is 2,880.

Gender Profile

The general profile of the respondents in six states reveals that they were predominantly male in all the States. In the entire sample of 2880 respondents selected out of six States, 75.3 percent were male. The proportion of females was the lowest in Uttar Pradesh at merely 15.8 per cent while Chhattisgarh had the highest proportion of women respondents at 41.7 per cent.

Table 7: Gender of Respondents

States	*Male*	*Female*	*Others*
Bihar	339 (70.6)	141 (29.4)	0 (0.0)
Chhattisgarh	276 (57.5)	200 (41.7)	4 (0.8)
Jharkhand	393 (81.9)	87 (18.1)	0 (0.0)
Madhya Pradesh	358 (74.6)	122 (25.4)	0 (0.0)
Odisha	400 (83.3)	80 (16.7)	0 (0.0)
Uttar Pradesh	402 (83.8)	76 (15.8)	2 (0.4)

N=480

Social Profile

Since districts with high proportion of socially backward communities were chosen, a large proportion of the respondents were Scheduled Castes and Scheduled Tribes. The overall profile of the respondents indicates that 74.2 per cent of respondents were Scheduled Castes and Scheduled Tribes. With the exception of Chhattisgarh, which had a majority of 51.7 percent of respondents belonging to Other Backward Castes, all the other States had a large majority of respondents belonging to SCs and STs. Uttar Pradesh had the highest proportion of SC/ST respondents at 91.8 per cent, with 88.3 percent of the respondents being SC alone. Odisha had the highest proportion of ST respondents at 68.5 per cent while it had the lowest proportion of SC respondents at 14 per cent.

With only two respondents, Bihar had a negligible proportion of ST respondents, thought it had a majority of 60.8 percent of SC respondents. The proportion of SC/ST respondents in Jharkhand and Madhya Pradesh was also substantially large with 88.5 per cent and 76 per cent respectively. The general castes and other communities constituted very small proportions in all the States.

Table 8: Social Profile of Respondents

States	*St*	*Sc*	*Obc*	*General*	*Other**
Bihar	2 (0.4)	292 (60.8)	178 (37.1)	8 (1.7)	0 (0.0)
Chhattisgarh	117 (24.4)	99 (20.6)	248 (51.7)	11 (2.3)	5 (1.0)
Jharkhand	241 (50.2)	184 (38.3)	47 (9.8)	8 (1.7)	0 (0.0)
Madhya Pradesh	181 (37.7)	184 (38.3)	81 (16.9)	28 (5.8)	6 (1.3)
Odisha	329 (68.5)	67 (14.0)	84 (17.5)	0 (0.0)	0 (0.0)
Uttar Pradesh	17 (3.5)	424 (88.3)	28 (5.8)	10 (2.1)	1 (0.2)

N=480 *Other Groups Who Do Fall In Any Category

Religious Profile

Religious composition of the respondents is important to understand the impact of MGNREGA across different religious communities. The respondents were found to be predominantly Hindu. In Madhya Pradesh, the respondents belonging to Hindu communities were 97.9 per cent which was the highest among all the other States. Interestingly, in Jharkhand, Hindus accounted for only 58.3 per cent of the respondents, which was the lowest among all the six States. However, 38.8 per cent of the respondents from Jharkhand claimed that they adhered to the Sarna religion, which is the faith of the tribals in the region. Barring Chhattisgarh, which had only one respondent adhering to Sarna faith, other States had no respondents of the Sarna faith. Only 4 per cent of the respondents were Muslims in Bihar and Uttar Pradesh, while other States had negligible proportion of Muslim respondents. In Odisha, there was not a single Muslim respondent, but 15.6 per cent of the respondents were Christians, which was the highest among all the States. Bihar and Madhya Pradesh (MP) had no Christian respondent, while other States had very small proportions of Christian respondents. There was only one respondent each belonging to Sikh, Jain and Buddhist religion in all the States.

Table 9: Religious Affiliation of Respondents

States	*Hindu*	*Muslim*	*Christian*	*Sarna*	*Others*
Bihar	461 (96.0)	19 (4.0)	0 (0.0)	0 (0.0)	0 (0.0)
Chhattisgarh	458 (95.4)	5 (1.0)	14 (2.9)	1 (0.2)	2 (0.2)
Jharkhand	280 (58.3)	9 (1.9)	5 (1.0)	186 (38.8)	0 (0.0)
Madhya Pradesh	470 (97.9)	9 (1.9)	0 (0.0)	0 (0.0)	1 (0.2)
Odisha	405 (84.4)	0 (0.0)	75 (15.6)	0 (0.0)	0 (0.0)
Uttar Pradesh	460 (95.8)	19 (4.0)	1 (0.2)	0 (0.0)	0 (0.0)

N=480 * Others Include 1 Sikh & 1 Jain In Chhattisgarh, And 1 Buddhist In Mp.

Educational Profile

The Educational Attainment Levels Of The Respondents Indicate That They Have Attained Very Poor Educational Qualifications. Primary Data On The Educational Status Reveal That 62.5 Per Cent Of The All The Respondents From All The States Were Illiterate. Besides, In Every State, The Majority Of Respondents Were Illiterate.

Table 10: Educational Attainment of Respondents

States	*Illiterate*	*Primary upto 5th Std.*	*Middle School*	*Matriculation*	*Inter-mediate*	*Graduate*	*Post-Graduate*
Bihar	405 (84.4)	38 (7.9)	19 (4.0)	15 (3.1)	3 (0.6)	0 (0.0)	0 (0.0)
Chhattisgarh	263 (54.8)	114 (23.8)	54 (11.3)	23 (4.8)	19 (4.0)	3 (0.6)	4 (0.8)
Jharkhand	287 (59.8)	86 (17.9)	46 (9.6)	34 (7.1)	22 (4.6)	5 (1.0)	0 (0.0)
Madhya Pradesh	267 (55.6)	74 (15.4)	69 (14.4)	31 (6.5)	19 (4.0)	12 (2.5)	8 (1.7)
Odisha	314 (65.4)	117 (24.4)	26 (5.4)	16 (3.3)	6 (1.3)	1 (0.2)	0 (0.0)
Uttar Pradesh	265 (55.2)	95 (19.8)	54 (11.3)	38 (7.9)	18 (3.8)	6 (1.3)	4 (0.8)

N=480

Highest illiteracy was found to be in Bihar with as many as 84.4 per cent of the respondents found to be illiterate in addition to another 11.9 per cent of the respondents being school drop-outs. Interestingly, lowest levels of illiteracy among respondents were noticed in Chhattisgarh, which had 54.8 per cent of its respondents illiterate, though it also had 35.1 per cent of respondents who were school drop-outs. As far as higher education goes, Bihar was the only State with not a single graduate among its respondents, while Jharkhand and Odisha had no post-graduate among its respondents. Madhya Pradesh had 4.2 per cent of its respondents, who had completed their graduation, while other States had miniscule proportion of graduates among their respondents.

Occupational Profile

The predominant occupation of the respondents in all the States is agriculture as 55 per cent of all the respondents in all the States are reported to be engaged in agriculture. Odisha has the largest number of respondents engaged in agriculture at 81.7 per cent compared to other States. Madhya Pradesh has the lowest proportion of respondents engaged in agriculture, but it also has the highest proportion respondents engaged as informal labourers (32.7 per cent) and the highest proportion of unemployed population at 35.4 per cent. The proportion of unemployed respondents was also high in Uttar Pradesh (24.5 per cent) and Chhattisgarh (22.9 per cent). The proportion of respondents engaged in other occupations such as animal husbandry, business, private service, etc. was not significant. The number of respondents who are students and retired people were reported to have been negligible.

Table 11: Main Occupation of Respondents

Occupation	*Bihar*	*Chhattisgarh*	*Jharkhand*	*Madhya Pradesh*	*Odisha*	*Uttar Pradesh*
Agriculture	228 (47.5)	256 (53.3)	311 (64.8)	117 (24.4)	392 (81.7)	282 (58.8)
Animal Husbandry	12 (2.5)	6 (1.3)	0 (0.0)	14 (2.9)	5 (1.0)	5 (1.0)
Business	25 (5.2)	7 (1.5)	20 (4.2)	8 (1.7)	18 (3.8)	24 (5.0)
Private Service	2 (0.4)	7 (1.5)	10 (2.1)	6 (1.3)	1 (0.2)	48 (10.0)
Student	3 (0.6)	4 (0.8)	0 (0.0)	4 (0.8)	0 (0.0)	1 (0.2)
Retired	2 (0.4)	6 1.3)	0 (0.0)	3 (0.6)	0 (0.0)	4 (0.8)
Unemployed	22 (4.6)	110 (22.9)	12 (2.5)	170 (35.4)	9 (1.9)	116 (24.2)
Labourers	0 (0.0)	76 (15.8)	127 (26.5)	157 (32.7)	55 (11.5)	0 (0.0)

N=480

Land Holding

The land holding pattern of the respondents reveals that they are largely landless or marginal farmers. It is pertinent to note that 52 percent of all the respondents were landless, thus making the implementation of MGNREGA very crucial for the livelihood security of the rural population. Another

31.9 per cent of the respondents from all the States were reported to be small farmers owning less than 2 acres of land.

Table 12: Land Holding Pattern of Respondents

Land Holding	*Bihar*	*Chhattisgarh*	*Jharkhand*	*Madhya Pradesh*	*Odisha*	*Uttar Pradesh*
Landless	335 (69.8)	295 (61.5)	152 (31.7)	351 (73.1)	130 (27.1)	237 (49.4)
<2 acres	83 (17.3)	95 (19.8)	248 (51.7)	79 (16.5)	221 (46.0)	192 (40.0)
2-4 acres	23 (4.8)	36 (7.5)	61 (12.7)	34 (7.1)	95 (19.8)	32 (6.7)
4-10 acres	18 (3.8)	13 (2.7)	16 (3.3)	13 (2.7)	34 (7.1)	17 (3.5)
>10 acres	11 (2.3)	4 (0.8)	3 (0.6)	0 (0.0)	0 (0.0)	1 (0.2)

N=480

Madhya Pradesh had the highest proportion of landlessness with 73.1 per cent of the respondents being landless. Landlessness was also high among respondents in Bihar (69.8 per cent) and Chhattisgarh (61.5 per cent). Odisha had the lowest proportion of landlessness compared to other States with only 27.1 per cent of the respondents being landless. However, Odisha had the highest proportion of respondents who were small farmers (46 per cent), marginal farmers owning 2-4 acres of land (19.8 per cent) and medium farmer owning 4-10 acres of land (7.1 per cent). Interestingly, Bihar accounts for the highest proportion of respondents, who are large farmers owning more than 10 acres of land, among all the other States covered in this study.

Annual Income

The economic profile of the respondents reveals a grim picture. The household income of over two-thirds of all the respondents is less than Rs. 65.8 per day, which is less than the international poverty level of $ 1.25 per day. The respondents in Odisha are the poorest with 89.6 per cent of them earning not more than 24000 in the whole year. The annual income of 82.9 per cent of the respondents in Madhya Pradesh fall the same category. The annual income of over two-thirds of the respondents in Uttar Pradesh and Chhattisgarh, and a majority of respondents from Bihar and Jharkhand also do not exceed Rs. 24,000. Except three respondents from Chhattisgarh, the annual income of all the other respondents from all the States does not exceed Rs. 48,000. The low income levels of the respondents indicate that the implementation of MGNREGA can be of great help to increase income levels of the rural poor.

Table 13: Annual Income of Respondents

Annual Income	*Bihar*	*Chhattisgarh*	*Jharkhand*	*Madhya Pradesh*	*Odisha*	*Uttar Pradesh*
12000 & below	19 (4.0)	155 (32.3)	75 (15.6)	209 (43.5)	203 (42.3)	152 (31.7)
12000-24000	230 (47.9)	182 (37.9)	175 (36.5)	189 (39.4)	227 (47.3)	168 (35.0)
24000-36000	112 (23.3)	88 (18.3)	154 (32.1)	39 (8.1)	46 (9.6)	106 (22.1)
36000-48000	85 (17.7)	52 (10.8)	76 (15.8)	42 (8.8)	4 (0.8)	52 (10.8)
48000 & above	0 (0.0)	3 (0.6)	0 (0.0)	0 (0.0)	0 (0.0)	0 (0.0)

N=480

The profile of the respondents from all the six States in which the study of the implementation and impact of MGNREGA is being undertaken reveals that they come from very poor socio-economic backgrounds. Though the respondents are largely male belonging to Hindu communities, a significant number of Scheduled Castes and Scheduled Tribes have been interviewed to understand whether MGNREGA is reaching the poorest of the poor in the six States. Primary data has confirmed that with the majority of the respondents being illiterate, landless and below poverty levels, the implementation of MGNREGA has the potential of improving the livelihood of the rural poor.

Chapter - III

Literature Survey

In order to ensure work security and wage security to the rural masses, MGNREGA was enforced in the economically backward districts with effect from 2nd February 2006. This chapter is an exhaustive search of relevant literature which is based on some published materials and some previous studies conducted on different aspects under Mahatma Gandhi National Rural Employment Guarantee programme.

Background

Ramanujam et. al (1998)[1] explained according to the estimates of the National Sample Survey Organisation, the number of unemployment people in the country in 1992 was 23 million and this had become 58 million backlog in 1997 and the backlog was expected to touch the mark of 94 million by 2002. The unemployment included both open and underemployment. The estimates for under employment could be obtained by subtracting the unemployment rate as per the usual principal status definition from the current status definition. In rural areas, open unemployment had been declining faster when compared with the overall position. But underemployment had been increasing marginally. He also highlighted some trends in the unemployment levels according to the gender, occupation and educational levels. He observed that educated unemployment was much higher in the rural areas that too among the females. Another important point made by Ramanujam et al. related to the casualisation of employment. According to him, casual employment had gone up from 23.4 per cent in 1972-73 to 35.6 per cent in 1993-94. The casualisation of employment would lead to lower skills, resulting in poor quality of work and lower wages. Though 65 per cent of the labour force was engaged in agriculture, the rate of agriculture growth was very low. Some of the future strategies at the macro level could include the improvement in the quality of employment provided. The employment created needed to be basically productivity-oriented and to achieve this, the skills of the people concerned could be integrated with technological factors. The other suggested course of action was involving females in a larger measure in the employment generation programmes and these two issues would mean spelling out a Human Resource Development Policy for the future. The reasons identified by him for a higher rate of unemployment included excessive dependence on agriculture, low growth rate of agriculture and marginal farmers entering the labour class.

Karunakaran (1998)[2] observes that focusing on non-agricultural employment in the rural areas would be crucial to poverty reduction. There is a correlation between the employment in both agricultural, non-agricultural sectors and poverty levels. The shrinkage in the agricultural employment would normally lead to increase in the employment in non-agricultural sector which would result in the decline of the poverty level. Promotion of agricultural growth in the form of improving irrigational facilities through watershed development programmes would result in non-agricultural growth. Non-governmental organizations have a critical role to play in the area of market development. It was also felt that highly professionalized marketing system for the tiny industry would go a long way in achieving the desired results.

Devi's study (1986)[3] holds that one should not forget that the poor are really poor due to serious and real constraints which cannot be overcome overnight and there is a cumulative effect of disadvantage leading to deprivation and both of them leading to despondence and perhaps dependence at the end. It may also be essential to organize the identified poor, encourage their own leadership and get them involved in decision-making process which ultimately concern them with a view to avoiding the feeling of alienation and powerlessness and thereby create a sense of efficacy which is so crucial for the success of any poverty reduction programmes in future.

Srivastava and Singh (1987),[4] based on the Proceedings of Dialogical Session, 1985 have come to the conclusion that durable asset creation for strengthening economic infrastructure in rural area may provide long-term income-employment generation effect. Similarly, asset creation in terms of a large number of irrigation works will improve agriculture and will reduce the risk involved in cultivation and will lead to greater labour absorption.

According to Haque (1998),[5] historically, development of the non-farm sector follows automatically as a consequence of the farm sector. This, however, has not happened where agriculture has grown and continues to grow at a very high rate. The infrastructure is also highly developed. But no such development of the non-farm sector has taken place. He also emphasized the need for developing composite skills in the rural labour. Another question raised was regarding the quality of employment.

For most of the world, MGNREGS has been a unique phenomenon. It has a demand-driven design, rights-based structure and unprecedented scale of investment by the Union government. Many scholars, researchers, social activists, policy makers and analysts around the world have intensely studied its implementation. Several studies have shown that works under MGNREGS have been fruitful in providing livelihood and income security, increased food intake, decreased incidence of poverty and improved health outcomes. Bela Bhatia and Jean Drèze (2002),[6] based on their experience in Manika and Manatu in Latehar district, Jharkhand, assert that MGNREGS has become a matter of great interest in the rural areas, that there is growing awareness of the promise of "100 days of employment for every household" and widespread demand for job cards. Government officials such as BDOs and Panchayat Sevaks find themselves compelled to devote a considerable part of their work time to MGNREGS-related matters, due not only to orders from the top but also to rising pressures from below.

Under MGNREGA Cover

The Mahatma Gandhi National Rural Employment Guarantee Act (MGNREGA) is intended to give a legal guarantee of employment to anyone who is willing to do casual manual labor at the statutory minimum wage. Any adult who applies for work under NREGA is entitled to employment in public works within 15 days; otherwise, it is a state responsibility to provide them unemployment benefit. However, this entitlement is subject to some important limitations. For instance, the work guarantee applies in rural areas only, and it is limited to 100 days per household per year. MGNREGA is based on the principle of self-selection, and it is a step towards legal enforcement of the right to work, as an aspect of the fundamental right to live with dignity. NREGA also mandates 33 percent participation for women.

Khera and Nayak (2009)[7] used qualitative data collected on 1060 NREGA workers from 98 NREGA worksites spread across 10 sample districts from six north Indian states to examine the socio-economic consequences of NREGA for women workers. They report that significant benefit have already started accruing to women through better access to local employment, at minimum wages, with relatively decent and safe work conditions. Almost half of the NREGA women workers responded that had they not worked at the NREGA worksites, they would have worked at home or remained unemployed. Pankaj and Tankha (2010)[8] based on their descriptive analysis of a field survey of MGNREGA workers report that women as individuals have gained because of their ability to earn independently, made possible due to the paid employment opportunity under MGNREGA. They use information collected from 428 female NREGA workers from four northern states in India.

Haque (2011)[9] has concluded in his study of 13 states of India including Chhattisgarh that there were no technically educated persons in the team of social audit, who could understand the technicalities of work and as a result physical inspection of works and assets was generally conducted in a very non-professional manner. Report also indicates how large gaps between various entitlements and their actual realization by the rural worker exist due to extremely low level of awareness. On the other hand, writing about impacts of MGNREGS Haque says that there has been a decline in the incidence of migration of workers in several places in the post MGNREGS scenario. In some places it was observed that farmers have improved the irrigated area and changed the cropping patterns. But due to lack of coordination and convergence there has been hardly any planned effort to ensure productive utilization of whatever assets have been created.

MoRD (2010)[10], in its 'report to people' on MGNREGS describes convergence of different programs and establishing synergy between them by the government of Chhattisgarh. Report concluded that Chhattisgarh undertook convergence initiatives for optimizing the irrigation capacity of all the major, medium and minor projects. The district administration has weaved together the objectives of employment guarantee and overall objectives of the development schemes under state plan/non-plan and central plan in these sectors.

Awareness and Implementation

The Indian School of Women's Studies Department (ISWSD,2006)[11] highlighted lower level of awareness in terms of application of the works demanding job and eligibility under the act. The Comptroller and Auditor General (CAG) (2009)[12] reported that with a difference of 22% the level of unawareness of the project is higher (61%) than the level of awareness (39%) about the rights and privileges under the schemes in rural Odisha.

Looking at the issues from the perspective of social groups, the Centre for Science and Environment (CSE) did a comparative study in two states, MP and Odisha, and reported that with a small difference the awareness among the villagers in MP is higher than that of Odisha. Again, even though the villagers are aware of the existence of the act, there was very little awareness about the various provisions of the act. The study measures the disparity of awareness within different sections of society and found that the level of awareness among the ST and OBCs is much lower than the people belonging to the general category.

Mohanty (2012)[13] empirical findings from the district of Sundargarh in terms of level of awareness were not very much encouraging. He recorded a high degree of unawareness about modes of applying for a job, availing minimum wages and even demanding work.

National Federation of Indian Women (NFIW) (2008) did a study on the social economic empowerment of women under National Rural Employment Guarantee Act (NREGA) in four districts each from Chhattisgarh, MP, and Orissa. The study found that awareness on how to apply for job card and demand driven work was reportedly poor. At the same time, awareness about minimum wages has been found to be better. However, the study identified three major problems in the study areas: Low awareness and accessibility, delayed payment of wages (which was comparatively higher in the state of Odisha) and worksite's lack of facilities.

A study conducted by NFIW (2008)[14] in three central states of India including Chhattisgarh concluded that the awareness level of the worker about entitlements of MGNREGS was quite low. Created assets are of no use due to lack of awareness and management of funds. Worksite conditions were also found worse except availability of drinking water.

Focusing on lack of people's planning the study revealed that that there is little effort of professional staff at social mobilisation without which there is hardly any chance of NREGA emerging as a people-centred programme. In Rajnandgaon, Raigarh, Sarguja and Jashpur districts of Chhattisgarh, works focused mainly on activities for which standardised estimates were available. Work done on rural employment programmes in India is measured through the schedule of rates (SoR). This schedule provides rates at which labour power is measured in terms of monetary value. Workers are paid according to the value placed on their work by the SoR. What the government has overlooked is that the present SoRs are meant for a system that uses contractors and machines to carry out public works. These contractors, as a rule, do not pay statutory minimum wages to labour and get most of their work done through earth moving machines (the word "JCB" is now used as a term for digger-excavator engineering vehicles in the name of a company JC Bamford Excavators). In Rajnandgaon district, Chhattisgarh, there were reports that sarpanchs fear getting work done under NREGA and that the unemployment allowance will have to be given out of the sarpanchs' pockets. In Sarguja district of Chhattisgarh, 50 per cent of NREGA works that were to be implemented by line departments, were invariably found using machinery. But in Raigarh and Jashpur, the use of both contractors and machines came down following public protest against the same. In Chhattisgarh, monitoring and vigilance committees were found active in Raigarh and Jashpur. In Rajnandgaon, monitoring and vigilance systems are either not present or inactive. In Sarguja, the social audits conducted were far from satisfactory (Ambasta, et.al., 2008)[15].

The government's flagship programme under the National Rural Employment Act is aimed at countering some of the developmental woes of the Indian state in the backward regions. Banerjee, etal. (2010)[16] examine these issues through a case study of the NREGA in Chhattisgarh. The districts chosen were from the first 200 where the NREGA had been implemented from 2006 onwards. These villages were also under the influence of the Maoists. The developmental indicators had shown very clearly that Chhattisgarh lagged behind on every indicator. In terms of social groups it was stated that Dalits, Adivasis, nearly all Backward Castes and Muslims were marginalized whereas women were the most discriminated. Some of these developmental woes were supposed to be addressed by the NREGA. Three years since the inception of the programme, the results in these areas leave much to be desired. In terms of the most backward areas, one of the chronic problems has been joblessness. Also, a substantial portion of backward districts suffered from very low levels of agricultural productivity. The annual average days of employment (during 2008-09) per household (except those in NREGA-related works) were low in most of the studied regions. In particular, for the regions in Chhattisgarh it was in the range of 60 to 70 days. By contrast, it was observed that Chhattisgarh had done relatively better in terms of providing employment through NREGA as compared to the other states.

The Govind Bhallab Pant Institute of Social Sciences GBPISS (2008)[17] conducted a survey in selected villages of Surguja district of Chhattisgarh and survey report is convinced that the usefulness of the assets created through MGNREGS fund in most cases is limited to the benefit of a particular group of people or in some cases to a few individuals. Survey concludes that even the implementation of MGNREGS in the sample gram panchayats was not up to mark, but workers felt that MGNREGS had made their lives better. The MGNREGS extended solution to internal migration as the people of this region left home in pursuit of employment during months when there was no work.

The Sahbhagi Shikshan Kendra, Lucknow in its research on district Sitapur reported that, among the respondents 12 per cent were totally unaware about the MGNREG programme whereas 50 cent had very low level of information. Only seven per cent people could be graded as utilizers of opportunities. . Further, a Gram Sabha (village assembly) was organized and it was reported that47 per cent respondents answered 'yes', but were unable to provide any further details; 42 per cent denied about any such congregation and 11% were found totally unaware about entire process.

Hence, available literature establishes low awareness despite a well provisioned guideline of the programme.

Wage Rate and Work Days

The wage rate paid under MGNREGA was much lower than what had been prescribed under the Minimum Wages Act (MWA). States have the freedom to fix minimum wages. The job act as a law that "guarantees those at the bottom of the economic pyramid their basic entitlements". According to the Telegraph, the payment of minimum wages under the act "created a synergy" between the MGNREGA and Act. (The Telegraph, 2012)[18]

Dutta et al (2012)[19], analyses of National Sample Survey (NSS) data for 2009-10 confirms expectations that poorer states of India meet more demand for work under the MGNREGS. However the data shows the considerable unmet demand for work in the scheme in all states, and more so in the poorest ones, where the scheme is needed most. In Chhattisgarh 69 per cent of rural households wanted work in the scheme. Of these, 69 per cent got work; and 31 per cent household did not get job even after demanding under the scheme. For Chhattisgarh the average wage rate under the MGNREGS is Rs. 82 in the year 2009-10 and the casual labor market rate is Rs. 69 for the same period. The study suggests handling lower capacity in poor states and lower empowerment of poor people in effective manner.

Over five-crore workers under the scheme of MGNREG workers across the country will enjoy a 17 to 30 per cent rise in wages with their wage rate being linked with the Consumer Price Index for Agricultural Labour (CPIAL) with immediate effect. The government had hiked the wages on the basis of the provisions of the MWA (M), which promises 100 days of employment to households below the poverty level in a year (The Hindu, 2011)[20]

Though Chhattisgarh received an award for its excellence in implementing the National Rural Employment Guarantee Scheme (NREGS) from the union rural development ministry, the report by the Comptroller and Auditor General CAG on its performance, presents a very different picture. The report, said that the government was able to provide average employment of only 35 days per household in 2007-08. The Act guarantees 100 days of employment in a financial year to any registered rural household. This has to be provided within 15 days of the demand. "In many cases, it was not possible to ascertain whether employment was provided within 15 days. It also could not be ensured how many days of employment had been provided", the report said. The report adds that 22 public works had been carried out by other implementing agencies without the recommendation or selection by the Gram Sabha or Gram Panchayat. There are a large number of deficiencies in preparing muster rolls. There were delays, even up to 326 days, in payment of wages to nearly one lakh members, defeating the very objective of the Act. There were several instances where the wages were paid without signatures or thumb impressions, the report said. In a state like Chhattisgarh, where the rural population is 78 per cent, the CAG report was an eye opener (The Hindustan Times, 2009).[21]

Despite adequate funds being disbursed to states, quite a few of them have failed to provide jobs to rural households for 100 days as stipulated in the flagship employment guarantee scheme. It is the responsibility of state governments to provide 100 days of work under National Rural Employment Guarantee Act (NREGA). The Centre provides adequate funds to the States, but the national average of work-days for the last three years was only around 45. The NREGA guidelines are provided to states, but it is up to them to see that work is given to the rural poor and job cards are distributed properly to NREGA beneficiaries. States must also ensure that fake job cards are not distributed to the beneficiaries of the scheme. The states such as Madhya Pradesh and Chhattisgarh pay less than Rs 100 for jobs under NREGA (The Hindu, 2009).[22]

Chhattisgarh provided employment of just 35 days per household on an average in fiscal 2007-08 under NREGS that ensures 100 days of employment in a financial year to any registered rural household. "Employment is to be provided within 15 days of demand under the NREGS. The Chhattisgarh government spent Rs.2,070.65 crore (Rs.20.7 billion) during 2006-08 providing average employment of 41 days during 2006-07 and 35 days during 2007-08," said a report of the CAG for 2007-08 for Chhattisgarh. The CAG further remarked about the state of implementation of NREGS, a flagship scheme of the central government, in Chhattisgarh, saying: "It was observed that the details of employment provided and payments made were either not entered or incomplete in the employment registers and test checked job cards. The report also highlighted that a huge delay was made in payment of wages and several people were also deprived of unemployment allowance (New Kerala, 2009)."[23]

Anxious to spur up the rural economy in the naxal-affected districts of the country, the Centre has underlined the imperativeness to implement NREGS in a more meaningful manner. Chhattisgarh was called upon to utilize the enhanced administrative expenditure to strengthen the implementation machinery. The department has directed the state to start at least one project work in each village and habitation and to provide cost of work tools to all the workers to avoid exclusion of asset-less workers and to ensure that wages were paid not later than a fortnight of the work done. The State was called upon to effectively adhere to the new provisions of convergence and enlargement of scope of NREGS for initiating development projects on the land of individuals belonging to the ST, SC, and Below Poverty Line (BPL) households, besides small and marginal farmers (The Hindu, 2009).[24]

Implementation Problems

Ambasta et al. (2008)[25] have pointed out some of the lacunae in implementation of MGNREGS like lack of professionals, understaffing, administrative delays, lack of people's planning, poor quality of work, inappropriate wage rates and poor social auditing. Datt (2008) reports that the main constraints are lack of professional staff, lack of project planning, bureaucratic resistance, inappropriate rates of payment, lack of worksite facilities and lack of transparency and social audit. Dhawan (2009) says that the current design of MGNREGS has left out some deserving women out of its purview. In as many as 10 states including UP and Bihar, women beneficiaries worked for less than 30 per cent of the mandated one hundred days. This was well below the national average of 40.60 per cent working days for women.

Chakraborty (2007)[26] stated that the NREGS (National Rural Employment Guarantee Scheme) had so far posed no problem for the budget. Its allocation is only marginally higher than what was spent in the past by the government on various rural employment programmes. It has been a demand-driven scheme and had fallen far short of meeting demand in some states. The fund utilisation ratio also varied widely across states. The NREGA was enacted in 2005 to provide a minimum guaranteed wage employment of 100 days in every financial year to rural households with unemployed adult members prepared to do unskilled manual work. In the past, public employment programmes in India targeted at the poor had been generally identified with poverty alleviation. The analysis by Chakraborty (2007) indicated that the existing institutional arrangement in poorer states was not good enough to implement the NREGA in an effective manner. The utilisation ratio was low in poorer states. So, there was an urgent need for both vertical and horizontal coordination across levels of governments within the states. It was felt that the gram sabha could play an active role in the planning, monitoring and supervision of activities under NREGA. At the same time it was felt that panchayats did not perform well in terms of management of the schemes in many instances. It was further stated that devolution of responsibilities and strict accountability norms would accelerate capacity building at the level of the panchayat and the scheme could effectively function as a demand-driven one. In assessing the demand for labour, panchayat level preparation of labour budgets would go a long way for effective implementation. Nevertheless, it needs to be emphasised that better coordination by the levels of governments with the gradual expansion of the programme covering more districts would lead to increased outlays and one would hope that the programme effectiveness will increase.

Other field studies corroborate the high workforce participation by the marginalized. A study conducted in five districts of Uttar Pradesh noted that in its sample, around 85 per cent of the beneficiaries belong to BPL, 50 per cent belong to SCs, and 45 per cent belong to the Other Backward Classes (OBCs) (Department of Extension Education 2007-08). In **Azamgarh district** More than 50 per cent of the beneficiaries under NREGA belonged to SC/ST households, i.e. about 54 per cent. Male workers from the households have dominated the scenario of NREGA activities as only from about 6 per cent families the female workers have come forward to participate.

Similarly Ashok Pankaj compared between Bihar and Jharkhand on the progress of MGNREGA. His assessment was that implementation was tardy and the effort was driven by the supply side. There was some improvement in Bihar in terms of livelihood security, work participation rate, reduction in distress migration and creation of community assets. Bihar had also put institutional arrangements on track and made provisions for separate staff for MGNREGA which had strengthened the implementation process. But mobilizing PRIs and civil society remained to be a dream. In Jharkhand the situation was more difficult due to political and administrative indifference and the lack of formal PRIs.

Banerjee et.al (2010)[27], in a study carried out in Maoist affected area of Jharkhand, Chhattisgarh and Orissa concluded that the underdevelopment and backwardness in the Indian context can largely be understood in terms of developmental paradigm followed by successive government. Socio-economic deprivation and exclusion have resulted in the growth of the Maoists in the backward areas of the country. The field survey of the study come to the finding that the charge that the Maoists have been blocking developmental schemes does not seem to hold much ground. The Maoists, however, have been blocking road construction but not the other kinds of permissible works under MGNREGS – specially, land development, small irrigation facilities, forestations etc.

Study has concluded that the task rate system is not explained properly to workers and moreover the different rates for different soil types are not implemented. The District Schedule of Rates in most backward districts is outdated. Study also had shown the increase in the overall employment and wages rate which resulted in increase in household income of the rural poor. As per the study of sample villages of Chhattisgarh, the net household income increase in the range of 160 per cent to 23 per cent in 2008-09 as compared to that in 2005-06. Study claims that, even though migration has not stopped entirely from these regions, the incidence of seasonal out-migration.

The rural job guarantee scheme may be floundering with the government admitting that the flagship programme suffers from delayed payments, poor awareness, lack of durable assets, faulty job cards and muster rolls. Some of the major criticisms of the MGNREGA enlisted endemic "lack of awareness about rights and entitlements" and inability of workers' to submit written applications as significant drawbacks. Patchy maintenance of records like job cards, dated receipts and incomplete muster rolls also indicate the scheme is not reaching beneficiaries or is prone to leaks and manipulation. Shortage of dedicated personnel is affecting the task of measuring and certifying completed works. It is also noted that "delay in wage payments and poor coverage of banks and post offices" alongwith "conduct and quality of social audits" are among major challenges experienced during implementation of the job scheme. More than five years after its rollout - during which it has been hailed for boosting the rural economy and being a buffer against extreme penury - opinion is more divided with calls for recasting the job scheme growing louder and some quarters insisting the programme embodied non-productive expenditure. A major lacuna is that MGNREGA funds are used for works of a non-permanent nature and this phenomenon diverts government spending from more productive sectors of the economy, the Finance Ministry's assessment mandates to "make assets more durable and productive." Without permanent assets, the money would evaporate. Other aspects of MGNREGA that need attention, according to the Ministry include slow grievance redress that is complicated by beneficiaries finding it difficult to approach authorities. The task becomes even more hazardous if those in office are responsible for malpractices in the first place (The Times of India, 2012)[28]

Not surprisingly, women's role in planning of assets under MGNREGA or conducting social audits of the implementation is not visible. During a recent survey of states **viz.** Chhattisgarh, Madhya Pradesh, and Odisha it was found that women workers did not take part in social audits. "An analysis of social audits reports conducted by NGOs in districts including Hardoi (UP), Surguja (Chhattisgarh), and Chitrakoot (UP) clearly indicate that the auditing processes have been mostly focused on issues such as registration of families, checking of muster rolls for preventing forgery, timely payment of wages and payment of unemployment allowance. It did not say anything about gram Panchayat's involvement in the implementation process" (CSE, 2008: 53)[29]

During a survey conducted by Participatory Research in Action (PRIA) in Sitapur (UP), women were discouraged from registering. The study by GBPSSI (2009) found that the statutory minimum requirement of 33 percent participation by women was not met in Chhattisgarh (25 percent), Jharkhand (18 percent), Bihar (13 percent) and UP (5 percent) (Quoted in Sengupta, 2009:219).

Ever since MGNREGA came into force, the cost of agricultural labour had gone up between 16 to 43 per cent depending on the nature of the soil and the crops. The agriculture ministry has therefore suggested to the Ministry of Rural Development that, MGNREGA be suspended during the period of high-crop activity so that labour can engage in sowing, transplantation and harvesting activities. A study conducted by the Kerala

University in Palakkad district confirms this viewpoint emphasising that rubber plantations and rice farmers have been affected due to labour shortage. Punjab sees a phenomenal rise in farm workers' prices during these months as demand is much higher than supply. Similarly, farmer unions in Andhra Pradesh warned of a 20 per cent drop in productivity during kharif in 2009 due to labour scarcity. This shortage has been found to cut across most states including UP, Bihar, Jharkhand and Chattisgarh (The Asian Age, 2011).[30]

If bringing wage employment to the rural poor was the idea behind the NREGS, the draft performance audit report of CAG points to a serious disconnect. Far from reaching the intended beneficiaries, the audit says the money has been diverted to NGOs and other implementing agencies. The four poorest states of Bihar, Orissa, Chhattisgarh and Jharkhand were anticipated to have a higher demand for employment, and accounted for 73 of the total 200 poorest districts selected for the NREGS in the first year. But in the "absence of identified low-wage areas", the CAG report says, the scheme has suffered from poor planning and hence "non-timely" provision of employment. The "lack of documentation" has also resulted in non-payment of minimum wages and denial of unemployment allowance, allowing "diversion" of funds. The NREGS hence is nowhere close to its goal of creation of durable infrastructure in rural areas, so as to contribute to long-term employment. While some may defend the lack of planning stating it was just the first year of implementation of the NREGS, the fact is that these districts were earlier covered under a different scheme where planning of projects was mandatory too. Some findings of the CAG's audit in Chhattisgarh – there had been no exact data on households which demanded work; job card numbers not mentioned in about 75 per cent of the projects being implemented through other agencies; wages paid at Rs. 58.73 per day as against rates of Rs. 61.37 per day and Rs. 62.63 per day, applicable during different periods. Works were allocated to other implementing agencies, which seldom sent any information regarding expenditure and employment provided (The Indian Express, 2008).[31]

State governments in general have desisted from paying unemployment allowances to BPL job-seekers under NREGA. At least that was the finding of a national study on the role of PRIs in the implementation of NREGA during April to December 2007 by an NGO, Society for Participatory Research in Asia (PRIA). As much as 68 per cent of the 4,680 households surveyed in 20 districts of 13 States covered by the NREGA had not been provided with a job within the stipulated period of 15 days as specified under the law. The States surveyed were Bihar, Chhattisgarh, Jharkhand, MP, Orissa, and UP. The reason was these States were unwilling to dole out the money. Secondly, such payments reflected poorly on the performance of the state and the officials concerned, who could invite penal action (The Hindu, 2008)[32]

The paper says that it is not possible to realise the massive potential of NREGA if we set out the same structure of implementation that has institutionalized corruption, inefficiency and non-accountability into the very fabric of Indian democracy. In Raigarh, Sarguja and Rajnandgaon districts of Chhattisgarh, uncertainty of tenure and resulting discontinuity have had an adverse impact on NREGA work. Project Officers are not motivated and feel that the work done by them has come to nothing. The documentation and procedural requirements of NREGA often make it undesirable as compared to these other schemes where financial leakages are noticed. Thus, the whole process of planning and design of works, implementation, measurement and payment is marked with poor attention to quality and long delays. In Chhattisgarh, the situation was found no different (Ambasta, et al, 2008).[33]

The corruption is plaguing implementation of its flagship programme MGNREGA and there is a need to address the issue meaningfully. Though the achievements of MGNREGA have been impressive, there have been issues with regard to its implementation that need to be recognised and addressed meaningfully. There has been public concern over misappropriation of funds and resources in MGNREGA. Measures such as notification of Social Audit Rules, which makes it mandatory to have a social audit conducted by Gram Sabha and asking CAG (Comptroller and Auditor General) to conduct a performance audit of MGNREGA, would help address the concerns of corruption. While implementation remains uneven and patchy across states and districts, there is evidence to suggest that MGNREGA has contributed to increased rural wages everywhere, reduced distress migration from traditionally migration-intensive areas, usage of barren areas for cultivation, and empowerment of the weaker sections and giving them a new sense of identity and attributing them with bargaining power. The study said works carried out under MGNREGA have led to a rise in groundwater, improvement in soil quality and reduction in vulnerability of production systems to climate variability. Micro-level studies indicate that the water conservation structures, desilting of traditional water bodies, plantations and other works taken up in MGNREGA, have improved water percolation and helped recharge groundwater (MoRD, 2012)[34]. This has also led to a rise in groundwater levels and water availability, increasing the area under irrigation in some cases, the study said. It says that an application of excavated silt from MGNREGA works has the potential to add to soil fertility. In Chittoor (Andhra Pradesh (AP)), excavated silt was applied to 36,000 acres of degraded lands belonging to SCs, STs and BPL families. This increased the soil fertility in terms of nutrients found in the soil. Croplands that had been treated by silt excavated from water bodies, recorded a two to three-fold increase in the organic carbon content. Observing that MGNREGA creates green jobs that contribute to environmental sustainability, the study said the rural job scheme is directly related to climate change mitigation and adaptation activities (The Financial Express, 2012).[35]

Saho (2007)[36] reported NREGA in Orissa quoting a study carried out by New Delhi-based Centre for Environment and Food Security (CEFS), in its survey to evaluate and assess the performance of NREGS in 100 Orissa villages, revealed that there is participatory loot and plunder of NREGS fund.

Vilam Singh, 26, a tribal daily wager getting Rs.122 a day under a job guarantee scheme in Chhattisgarh was reported to own 74 acres of double-crop farm land, according to a state Congress leader and former minister. He had bought the land in phases between July 2010-Jan 2011 in neighboring Janjgir-Champa district in an area where a private power company was setting up a coal-fired power plant. Vilam Singh, who came from the Pandariya assembly constituency, was reported about his economic status that his family had been reeling under severe poverty. In fact, they struggled for food for years. It was informed that he was used as a 'cover' by a power company to purchase several local tribals' lands in his name to set up its plant by evading the land law existing in the state regarding tribals. And also to avoid high land compensation and rehabilitation package applicable for the use of private land for industrial purposes. According to the law in the state, the sale of tribals' land to non-tribals was prohibited, and requires special permission of the district collector. Any land acquisition also entails compensation and rehabilitation to the affected tribals. A probe was sought into the matter by the Central Bureau of Investigation (CBI) in this regard (New Kerala, 2011).[37]

Ashok Pankaj (2012)[38] compared Bihar and Jharkhand on the progress of MGNREGS. His assessment was that implementation was tardy and the effort was driven by the supply side. There was some improvement in Bihar in terms of livelihood security, work participation rate, reduction in distress migration and creation of community assets. Bihar had also put institutional arrangements on track and made provisions for separate staff for the scheme, which had strengthened the implementation process. But mobilizing PRIs and civil society remained a dream. In Jharkhand the situation was more difficult due to political and administrative indifference and the lack of formal PRIs.

According to Sood (2006), in Jashpur block (Chhattisgarh), lack of staff is having a negative impact. The sub-engineer had to maintain job cards. Such additional tasks could be farmed out to the youth of the village. According to official data presented by Dr. Y.B. Prasad (Xavier Institute of Social Service, Ranchi) at a workshop held in Ranchi on 29 May 2006, 1.5 lakh applications for job cards have been rejected in the state. The reason for rejection was that the applicant household had not been listed in the BPL Census 2002.

According to Maulick (2009), there was delay in distribution of job cards. Beneficiaries were wrongly selected. Needy households were not reached. There were, besides, the problems of understaffing, administrative delays, lack of people's planning, poor quality of work undertaken and poor social audit process. According to Tripathi (2009), eighteen-year-old Manoj, a dalit, swelled with hope when his Gram Sabha announced MGNREGS, but after working for MGNREGS for two months he got paid only for 28 days, and after a long delay. He feels that it is better to work as farm labour which at least gets him Rs 34 to 40 at the end of the day. There were also complaints of caste and communal bias in enrolment. In Barabanki district of UP *(Uttar Pradesh),* activists have been able to mount pressure on the administration to act.

According to Siddharthaand Vanaik (2008)[39], muster rolls are almost never present at the worksite, in Orissa. Muster rolls examined by the survey team often had fake names or inflated entries. The job card design was faulty to the point of being useless (e.g. it had no columns to record wage payments). Contractors were found at nearly half of the sample worksites.

In Reva district, Madhya Pradesh, Jain (1989) reported problems of inadequate staff, lack of accountability, inadequate employment generation, inadequate coverage of the scheme, lack of productive and technological works, inefficient management of work, and involvement and misbehaviour of contractors. According to the National Tribunal (2006), in one district tremendous hurdles were faced at the first stage of registration and acquiring of the job cards. Women-headed households and joint families are mainly disadvantaged.

Parshuram Rai (2007)[40] did a survey in 100 villages across six districts in Kalhandi Bolangir Koraput (KBK) region of Odisha (Bolangir, Nuapada, Kalahandi, Koraput, Nabrangpur and Rayagada) and the findings of the survey reveals flaws in the system of implementation. The study claimed that out of Rs.733 crore spent during the year, almost 75% of the amount had been siphoned off, which is amounting to the tune of Rs. 500 crore. A case was filed in the Supreme Court of India and the case (writ Petition civil-645 if 2007) is still going on. After hearing the case and looking into the gravity of the allegation, the apex court directed the CBI to inquire into the matter (12th May 2011). The CBI report and the final judgment are awaited.

Dreze (2007)[41] surveyed thirty randomly selected Panchayats in three districts of western Orissa (Boudh, Bolangir, Kalahandi). The survey included careful verification of muster rolls of a randomly selected NREGA work in each of this Gram Panchayat. His report reveals about the corruption in rural employment programs in Odisha and how this has continued in MGNREGs as well. However, he believes that there is tremendous potential of MGNREGA in the survey areas. Where work was available, it was generally found that workers earned close to and sometimes more than the statutory minimum wage of Rs.70 per day, and that wages were paid within 15 days or so. Based on the above study, Dreze et. al [42] identified 10 loopholes in NREGA Odisha, these are – (1) the faulty design of cards, (2) erratic maintenance of job cards, (3) incomplete distribution of job cards, (4) adjustment in muster rolls and job cards, (5) lack of transparency in muster rolls, (6) rigid management of information systems, (7)continued hold of contractors (middlemen), (8) vulnerability to local collusion, (9) cryptic work measurements and (10) other vulnerabilities like staff shortages, dormant Gram Sabhas, ritualistic vigilance procedures, and lack of grievance redressal.

Nayak, Behera andMishra[43] did their study in 2 districts of Orissa viz. Mayurbhanj and Balasore, and reported that both the districts have achieved certain goals and failed in others. The study shows that the two sample districts are good in certain physical and financial parameters like provision of employment to those who demand jobs and maintenance of wage and non-wage ratio. However, their performance in certain other important parameters like utilization of funds and creation of demand for jobs are not very encouraging. While the target is to guarantee 100 days employment to each household, not many households have achieved this target. According to this report well thought out effort is necessary to address these problems of NREGA in the state.

Mahapatra (2010)[44] did a cross state analysis of women's participation in MGNREGA and found some unique and often contradicting aspects. His analysis was between the states sharing low casual women workforce (Kerala, Tamil Nadu, Rajasthan) and States sharing high casual women workforce (Odisha, Uttar Pradesh and Bihar) and reached to a contradictory finding that the states having low share of women workforce has higher participation in MGNREGA (varies 69% to 82%) whereas the states where share of the women in workforce high has reportedly low participation (22-23%) in the programme. This finding is contradictory to the assumption that poverty forces women take up casual jobs. At the same time his findings show that participation of women in MGNREGA has been growing since its inception.

Mohanty (2012)[45] in his MA dissertation on Humanities and Social Science has tried to examine critically the implementation process of the program and its impact on tribal livelihoods in Sundargarh district of Odisha. The findings of his study show that the faulty implementation strategy has ruined the spirit of the program. The study also reported that in the district religion, street biasness and favoritism seem to influence the distribution of job card.

Baisakh assessed the performance of MG-NREGA over a period of 5 years (2006-2012).[46] He used extensively the available official data from the NREGA website and then compared the state with other states in terms of expenditures, families having job cards, number of days at work. His analysis concluded that MGNREGA performed badly in the poverty stricken districts of Odisha.

Under MGNREGA various activities that were being notified are implemented in the state. During the initial year of implementation rural connectivity was given much more emphasis. Other activities like drought proofing, water conservation and other activities are carried out in the state as well. "Farm Pond" is a special and state specific programme implemented by the State government for poor BPL, Indira Awaas Yojana beneficiaries, ST and SC families and beneficiaries of land reform families. The state had been targeting the schemes and has gone to the extent of announcing to excavate 5 lakh farm ponds in 5 years. Later "Mo Pokhari"- multipurpose Farm Pond is launched as special programs, meant for the small and marginal farmers (having 5 acres of land). This is also taken up in a targeted mode. Both these schemes are meant for poor families having land. There was criticism about the nature of targeting of these special state specific schemes.

Critics were of the opinion that it is undermining the spirit "participatory and demand driven nature" of the MGNREGA.

A study by Birner, et.al. (2010)[47] looks at implementation process of MGNREGA, based on two districts of Bihar and indicates the problems of governance issues in implementation. It argues how elite captures the power structure and change not only the systemic character but also the definition of government's projects. Exclusion in issuing of job cards, lack of awareness and capacity among rural citizens, misappropriation of funds, lack of capacity due to staff shortages and lack of training are some of the important aspects of MGNREGA in Bihar which this study has revealed.

Thus, the main problems in implementation of MGNREGS are definition of a household, denial of registration, delay in distribution of job cards, fees being charged for work application forms, non-issuance of receipts, absence of worksite facilities, non-availability of muster rolls at worksite, shortage of staff, delay in appointments, non-availability of regular works, delay in wage payment and payment of less than the minimum wage (Kohli, 2009).

Impact

Reviewing the National Rural Employment Guarantee Programme (NREP), Jha, et. al, (2008)[48], in their paper present the results on the participation of rural workers in NREG based on a pilot survey. The focus is on participation in the NREG programme of different socio-economic groups and the determinants of the participation of these groups. It was found that the mean participation was 59 days and that targeting was satisfactory. The performance of the programme had been far from dismal. Econometric evidence further confirms that the targeting was satisfactory. The disadvantaged groups of 'the landless households, had significantly high probabilities of participating in NREG thus, corroborated the buoyancy of Dreze (2007)[49] and Roy et al. (2008).[50] This, however, should not be taken to imply that relatively affluent households were screened and excluded. In fact, the probability of participation was higher in households owning moderate quantities of land or among the self-employed in agriculture. Thus, the critics of the NREG programme were correct that the performance has not been uniformly successful. Considerable more work needs to be done, as Roy et al. (ibid) rightly stated, to ensure sound planning and to overcome political apathy. Even if the focus was on duration of participation in the programme, measured by the number of days worked, an important result was that the higher the probability of participation, the longer was the duration of participation. Also even within the same district, there were significant village effects in both participation and duration of participation in the NREG programme.

Society for Regional Research and Analysis (SRRA) (2010)[51] in its study of migration among STs in Chhattisgarh, MP, Jharkhand and Orissa has observed that, circular migration, or rural-urban migration, and distress migration are emerging as a dominant form of migration amongst STs in India. On the other hand a large majority of migrant tribal women and girls and their families are unaware of the tribal development programmes of the government. Study strongly recommends sustained availability of work at the grass root level.

Khan and Saluja, 2007, in a study of NREGA ensures that demand for the employment in the programme has been particularly low in poorer states, such as Bihar, Orissa and UP which have a high incidence of out-migration for work. In short, it is widely acknowledged that on the whole, labour migration has not decreased significantly since NREGA came into effect (Khan and Saluja 2007; Das 2008; Jacob 2008) and a number of explanations for this have been advanced.

There is extensive literature demonstrating the importance of MGNREGA in India's rural development. These studies can be mainly categorized in two different segments: firstly, focus is on the potential of NREGA, which includes quite a significant number of literatures that are mainly based on the massive potential of the reforms suggested in NREGA. Most of these studies have examined the operational efficiencies of the NREGA. Secondly, the impact on rural households, wherein, the academicians and policy makers have also taken increased interest in assessing the impact of MGNREGA on the rural households from different aspects, namely, awareness, impact on the livelihoods, women empowerment, rural-urban migration, agricultural wages, marginalized sections, implementation problems, and so on.

Drèze and Oldiges (2009)[52] point to an increase in the participation of women (from 40 percent in 2006-7 to 44 percent in 2007-8). Large inter-state variations in the participation of women have been observed: more than two-thirds in states such as Kerala (71%), Rajasthan (69%) and Tamil Nadu (82%) and less than the stipulated one-third in states like Bihar (27), Uttar Pradesh (15), and Jharkhand (27)]). Other work on NREGA has highlighted the various benefits accruing to women from NREGA.

A number of literature based on empirical studies are available on the role of NREGA in achieving livelihood security and promoting sustainable development. These studies depicts that NREGA programme has shown mixed results so far in whole rural India. Mathur (2007)[53] argues in favour of NREGA that it has marked the beginning of momentous changes in the lives of the rural poor. He shows that migration has reduced in several villages in Chhattisgarh and Orissa, was less than minimum wage were raised in many states, the participation of women increased significantly even in the districts of UP.

The GBPSSI (2009)[54] study of six north Indian states found that 73 percent of respondents belong to Scheduled Caste/Scheduled Tribe families. The CESS (2009) study reported that majority of NREGA beneficiaries came from the vulnerable social groups (SCs, STs, and OBCs), landless agricultural laborers, and women. The same study found that participation of SC and OBCs is more than their respective shares in the total households. Such conditions reflect the fact that the workers face multiple deprivations and hence NREGA work becomes an important source for sustaining them at the subsistence level. Even in Bihar, benefits reached mostly the target groups and the process was also found non-discriminatory (Sengupta, 2009:219). Majority of the NREGA workers belong to the most disadvantaged sections of the society. At the all India level, SC and ST families together account for over 55 per cent of the total employment days created. While there are annual variations interns of participation of STs there is a steady growth in the participation of SC families over the three year period (Sengupta, 2009:219).

Bhagwati of Gram Panchayat Khaira in Rajnandgaon district of Chhattisgarh, said, "Before NREGA we were forced to work as agricultural labourers or casual labourers in brick kilns for Rs. 25 to Rs. 30 per day. But under NREGA we are getting Rs. 62 to Rs. 64 per day, more than double, which is almost an unexpected amount for us," (Jandu, 2008).[55]

Due to implementation of NREGA, there was increase in both overall employment and wage rates which resulted in increase in household income of the rural poor. In the study regions of Chhattisgarh, the net household income increased in the range of 160 per cent to 23 per cent in 2008-09 as compared to that in 2005-06 (Banerjee, et.al., 2010).[56]

Women's role in planning or conducting social audits is not visible. During a recent survey of states (Chhattisgarh, MP, Orissa) it was found that women workers did not take part in social audits. "An analysis of social audits reports conducted by NGOs in districts including Hardoi (UP), Surguja (Chhattisgarh), Chitrakoot (UP) clearly indicate that the auditing processes have been mostly focused on issues such as registration of families, checking of muster rolls for preventing falsification, timely payment of wages and payment of unemployment allowance. It did not say anything about gram panchayat's involvement in the implementation process" (CSE, 2008).[57]

There have been many evaluation studies on the impact of NREGA on women. Based on field data of 1060 NREGA workers from states of North India, Khera and Nayak (2009)[58] studied the socio-economic consequences of NREGA for women workers. They observed that though there were drawbacks in Bihar, Chhattisgarh, Jharkhand, MP, Rajasthan and UP in implementation of the NREGA, it has started providing significant benefits to rural women by offering access to local employment at the statutory minimum wage with relatively decent and safe work conditions mostly in their own village. Taking different case studies, the study also observed that NREGA has helped in improving gender relations in some of the most remote areas of the country. Similarly, the impact of NREGA on women empowerment in four North Indian states revealed a direct impact of NREGA in increasing the social status of women. The study revealed that NREGA had benefited rural women in two ways: first, it has opened a new avenue of paid employment; and, second, it has broadened their choices and capabilities, by reducing dependence on other family members. It was also revealed that MGNREGA can also have a significant positive impact on reduction in child labour through income effects and women's wellbeing and empowerment. According to the study, the programme had increased income through higher wage rates, rise in agricultural wages, decline in migration, and so on.

The Society for Participatory Research in Asia (PRIA) has praised the Rajasthan government's recent initiative to increase women's participation in the NREGS by rewarding the women labourers who have completed 100 days of work in a financial year. The study was carried out under PRIA's programme titled "Governance where people matter". In addition to Rajasthan, the study was conducted in Bihar, Chhattisgarh, Jharkhand, MP, Orissa, and UP. Sample size and data collection was done at five levels – State, district, block, village panchayats and household. The study found that although a large number of households were getting employment under NREGS, they were "not getting it when they most needed it". A large number of households received their wage payment after a maximum period of 15 days. The data suggested that more than one-third of the households received less than minimum wages, although almost all registered households had been issued job cards. Village panchayats, designated as principal authorities for planning and executing NREGS, were facing difficulties because of non-availability of staff (The Hindu, 2009).[59]

These positive effects can in turn reduce child labour and increase the participation of children in education. The less privileged communities in India have also benefited from NREGA. A state wise analysis of the Act shows that, compared to the share of population in India of SCs and STs, their participation rates in NREGA have been much higher in almost all states. Similarly, NREGA, by guaranteeing employment, has also alleviated the problem of rural-urban migration. It is assumed that it has impacted both the seasonal and the permanent migration trends. Seasonal migrations were reduced because rural workers secured employment during the lean season at their home districts. Permanent migrations are also likely to have been reduced because of rural development (Drèze et, al, 2008).[60]

The NREGS mooted by the Union Government has ushered a windfall for many deprived villagers in Chhattisgarh. This ambitious NREGS programme was launched in 2006 to provide employment to the unemployed and landless villagers. For instance, this scheme has benefitted the residents of Kanchanpur village in Koriya district of Chhattisgarh to a great extent. Evident are the instances of these villagers being regularly employed as such their worries over hunting for jobs elsewhere have been literally erased. Now they don't have to venture out for their daily bread anymore. They are harnessing their productive potential to the hilt and are getting at least 100 days of employment, the output of which is dedicated to the overall rural development of their very own region. "Now we don't need to go elsewhere in search of work. We are getting work in our village. This way, we are making earning enough for our livelihood," said Siyaram Yadav, a villager. Under this scheme many other villagers in Koria district are being ensured of employment in various categories like land development, rural connectivity, water conservation and water harvesting among others. "Under the rural employment scheme, we are focusing on activities like land levelling, construction of wells, digging of new ponds. In afforestation category, we are providing employment in agriculture and horticulture activities," Koriya District Panchayat said (One India, 2009)[61]

Apart from its contribution to households, NREGA has had a beneficial impact on the community and village economy. Drèze et.al. 2007 found that 92 per cent of workers felt that the NREGA work was useful and 83 per cent felt that NREGA has led to useful assets creation. Most of these studies showed that the coverage of NREGA at the micro-level, i.e. at the panchayat and village levels, has varied within the country. In other words, the Act has varied impact across states.

Every year, around 40,000 children migrate from the Orissa alone, and help their parents in the brick kilns, perform all sorts of hazardous works living in perilous conditions and facing exploitations of all kinds, physical, mental and other abuses. The number usually goes up in a drought year. According to a report of the Samuhik Marudi Pratikar Udyaam, Padampur, around 20,000 people migrate from western Odisha and other parts of Chhattisgarh every year. Those who migrate to other parts of western Odisha to harvest paddy, also carry their children. And, those who migrate to Raipur (Chhattisgarh) to pull rickshaw to earn their livelihood, also carry their children. One-fourth of the total migrants constitutes the children. Migration has become a big business in western Odisha. As the poor get a huge amount of money at a time, they are migrating (The Pioneer, 2010)[62].

The NREGA, which entitles rural households to 100 days of casual employment on public works at the statutory minimum wage, contains special provisions to ensure full participation of women. This paper, based on fieldwork in six states in 2008, examines the socio-economic consequences of the NREG for women workers. In spite of the drawbacks in the implementation of the legislation, significant benefits have already started accruing to women through better access to local employment, at minimum wages, with relatively decent and safe work conditions. The paper also discusses barriers to women's participation. This paper presents some findings related to women NREGA workers from a field survey conducted in May-June 2008 in six north Indian states including Chhattisgarh. This paper highlights the significance of NREGA work in light of the fact that women have limited access to wage work. It is important to note that there are large variations in the female participation in the NREGA across sample areas. Overall, 32 per cent of the sample workers were women. In Chhattisgarh's Surguja district 25 per cent was the female workers' participation rate (Khera, et. al., 2009).[63]

Shankar, et.al (2012)[64] describes in a study of MGNREGS in three states viz., Andhra Pradesh, Tamilnadu and Rajasthan that despite of several problems the scheme has succeeded in helping the poor supplement their income. The SCs and STs have participated in large numbers in MGNREGS as they have been landless and poor.

Ministry of Rural Development (MoRD) (2010)[65], in a report of working group on 'Specific Needs of Special Categories under MGNREGA' pointed in terms of Left Wing Extremism (LWE) areas that despite limitations, the contribution of MGNREGS has been found to be beneficial and measures to strengthen MGNREGS would be more rewarding to the rural communities and more to the disadvantaged section. The group recommended for providing the training and skill development for self employment to literate youth as wage seekers under MGREGS, such as masonry, brick making, mobile repairs, book keeping, maintenance of muster roll etc. Siddhartha, et.al (2008)[66], quoting first performance audit of MGNREGS by CAG, highlights the necessity of formulating new "district-wise Schedules of Rates (SOR)" for the MGNREGS with carefully calibrated and realistic stipulated tasks so as to ensure fair payment of wages. The CAG report has also explained the reluctance of state governments to disburse unemployment allowances.

Convergence of the NREGS with other schemes in drought-hit areas may remain a promise. For, the Ministry of Rural Development (MRD) says it has no special convergence plan tailored to the needs of drought hit states. Convergence of NREGS has invited criticism from the civil society, as it is seen as a back-door effort to dilute NREGA and to divert funds meant for the payment of wages. The proposal to relax the number of work days in NREGA is expected to get the nod from the Empowered Group of Ministers (EGoM) on drought. The drought-affected states need to receive more funds under NREGA that would be made available to enhance the number of work days to 150. As for convergence with other schemes, the convergence guidelines drawn in 2009 could apply, and the emphasis could be on drought prevention works in such areas - though there has been no such directive from the ministry on this. Activists like Jean Dreze and Aruna Roy have staunchly opposed convergence. Another school of thought, represented by activists like K. S. Gopal, has favoured convergence of NREGA, especially with schemes under the Ministry of Agriculture. Gopal, however, says that convergence can be a back-door effort for fund diversion. However, the new guidelines or NREGA 2, which are yet to be notified, would expand the number of works and in this some convergence might be achieved (The Business Standard, 2012).[67]

Thus, the reforms suggested in the Act can potentially transform the livelihoods of the poorest, heralding a revolution in rural governance in India. Study by Chakraborty (2007)[68] examined empirically how various features of NREGA, such as, access in rural areas, work guarantee, wage level and limited participation period, has influenced the welfare situation of the individual households. According to these studies, NREGA has reduced the incidence of poverty in rural households through its impact on food security, income, savings and health outcomes (Ambasta et al. 2008)[69]. Kohli (2009) concludes that MGNREGS has improved the beneficiaries' diet (69 per cent), curbed migration (59 per cent), helped in sending children to school (38 per cent), facilitated coping with illness (50 per cent), enabled repaying debts (32 per cent) and rescued them from doing hazardous work (35 per cent). Women respondents (33 per cent) had no earnings except their MGNREGS wages. MGNREGS increased the general wage rate in the area to Rs. 85 per day. According to Kumar (2011), women's participation for FYP 2008-9 in MGNREGS was 48 per cent and that of SC and ST households was nearly 54.72 per cent. According to data compiled by the Ministry of Rural Development, in states like UP, and Odhisa, daily wage rates given to agricultural labourers have risen following the introduction of MGNREGS, from Rs. 65 two years earlier to Rs. 85 in 2009 (Sharma 2009).

Centre for Science and Environment (CSE)'s (2008)[70] two states' study including MP and Odisha, assess the potential impact of MGNREGA on the creation of natural resources asset base and the resulted impact of rural livelihood, food security, lifestyle charges, economic regeneration and the impact on rural-urban migration. The study also assessed the institutional aspects such as the process of decision making capacity building, building long term institutional structures. The study found that MGNREGA has done some good jobs in terms of water availability in the village, constructing link roads. Since, the availability of work is less than 100 days people are forced to migrate. In the same line Ronalisa Parida (Orissa Diary) shows his concern that MGNREGA is an initiative to discourage the distress migration of the rural laborers which is not getting demand impact, because of the provisioned 100 days employment only. Therefore, the scheme fails to address the seasonal unemployment which is quite high in the state of Odisha.

NFIW (2008)[71] reported that, despite numerous problems in MGNREGA implementation, it has brought many positive impacts on women's life like: capabilities to earn more, gaining respect in the society, figuring in the public sphere. Women were also found concerned about their children's education. Above all, many were made free from the clutches of local moneylenders and have started saving small amount. The CAG, (2009)[72] reported that, despite the implementation of NREGS in the Odisha state, the rural migration in the state has increased 116%. The report revealed that the rate of rural migration was abnormally high by 483 per cent in Nuapada district while the state average was 116%. Dreze (2007)[73] from his survey in western Odisha (mentioned above) found that there was a lot of hope among the workers from MGNREGA. It would enable them to avoid long-distance seasonal migration. Further, there was plenty of scope for productive MGNREGA works in this area, in the field of water conservation, rural connectivity, regeneration of forest land, or improvement of private agricultural land.

Institute of Applied Manpower Research (IAMR) (2007)[74] undertook an evaluation survey in 16 states from 5 zones, 20 districts. In Odisha, the study was undertaken in the districts of Sambalpur and Sundargarh. The study assessed the impact through income generation of the scheme. The findings of the study concluded with the rising trend of income among the households in the study area which further increased the expenditure pattern on food and non food items of the beneficiaries. Distress migration, though checked, was found higher in the eastern states than others. However, the study found an encouraging range of participation from the female headed households.

A study conducted by National Federation of Indian Women NFIW[75]" on "Socio-economic empowerment of women under NREGA" in selected districts of Chhattisgarh, Madhya Pradesh, and Odisha found out that there was enhanced women's identity and empowerment as NREGA provided an economic opportunity. Respondents in all the states have been found to be very optimistic about the importance of NREGA in their lives. Another aspect of understanding NREGA is the growing contribution of women workers to the sources of their households' livelihood. The study reveals that in spite of all the grey areas in the implementation of NREGA, a silent revolution is taking place in rural India with respect to women in disguise. The major findings of the study are that with NREGS, women workers are getting empowered as visible in the form of growing contributions to household expenditure, bearing cost of children's education and healthcare, women have also started to appear more actively in the rural public sphere as they take up their work and responsibilities. Moreover, there is a general trend of low migration in the areas where assessment was carried out. The workers have started to repay their debts. The study reveals that despite numerous problems, NREGA is a programme that has begun to make a difference in the lives of women. Furthermore, it is popular among the workers, who routinely ask if more work could be made available to them under the NREGA.

Notes

1. MSC Ramanujam, I.C. Awasthi & Gayatri Pande (1998). Rural employment:: past, present and future,., 1998, pp 40.
2. C. Karunakaran (1998). From the Compilation Fifty Years of Rural Development in India: Retrospect and Prospect, p. 41.
3. Pajula Devi. A.K.(November- December 1986). "Poverty in Rural Areas: A Study", Kurukshetra, Vol. XXXV, No. 2-3..
4. *Srivastava,M. and A.K. Singh (1987). Rural Development in India, New Delhi: Deep & Deep Publications.*
5. Haque, T. (1998). New Strategies for Mitigating Rural Poverty in fifty years of rural development in India. National institute of Rural Development, Hyderabad.
6. B. Bhatia & J. Drèze. (2006). "Employment Guarantee in Jharkand: Ground Realities." Economic and Political Weekly, 41 (29): 3198–3202.
7. Khera R and Nayak N. (31 March—2 April 2009). "Women Workers and Perceptions of the National Rural Employment Guarantee Act in India." Paper presented at the FAO-IFAD-ILO Workshop on Gaps, Trends and Current Research in Gender Dimensions of Agricultural and Rural Employment: Differentiated Pathways out of Poverty, Rome.
8. A. Pankaj,& R. Tanka. (2010). "Empowerment Effects of the NREGS on Women Workers: A Study in Four States." Economic and Political Weekly, 45 (30): 45–55.
9. T. Haque. (2011): 'Socio-economic impact of implementation of Mahatma Gandhi national rural employment guarantee Act in India', Social Change, 41 (3), p-445-447, New Delhi, India: Sage Publication..
10. Mahatma Gandhi National Rural Employment Guarantee Act 2005, Report to the People 2nd Feb 2006 To 2nd Feb 2010, Ministry of Rural Development Government of India. New Delhi.
11. ISWSD (2006) Monitoring and Evaluation of National Rural Employment Guarantee Scheme with Special Focus on Gender Issues, Indian School of Women's Studies Development: New Delhi.
12. Comptroller and Auditor General Report, March 31, 2009. http://ezinearticles.com/?Labour-Migration:-A-Shadow-of-Poverty-in-Orissa&id=115270, visited 31.1.2013.
13. Soumya Mohanty (2012). "Mahatma Gandhi National Rural Employment Guarantee Act and Tribal Lielihoods: A case Study in Sundargarh District of Odisha." Department of Humanitites and Social Sciences, National Institute of technology, Rourkela.
14. National Federation for Indian Women (2008), Socio-economic Empowerment of Women under NREGA, retrieved from www.ipc-undp.org/pressroom/files/ipc163.pdf.
15. Ambasta Pramathesh, P S Vijay Shankar, & Mihir Shah. (2008). Two Years of NREGA: The Road Ahead. Economic & Political Weekly.
16. Banerjee K and Saha P (2010), 'The NREGA, the Maoists and the Developmental Woes of the Indian State', Economic and Political Weekly, Vol. 55, no. 28, July 10, pp.42-47.

17. G.B. Pant Institute of Social Science (2008): 'Survey of the status of the National Rural Employment Guarantee Act (NREGA) in five sample Gram Panchayat (GPs) of Udaipur Block, Surguja District, Chhattisgarh', Allahabad. pp.1-15,
18. The Telegraph (22 January 2012).
19. P. Dutta, Rinku Murgai, Martin Ravallion, & Dominique van de Walle (2012), 'Does India's Employment Guarantee Scheme Guarantee Employment?'. Economic and Political Weekly, Vol. No. p. 55-64.
20. The Hindu (7 January 2011).
21. The Hindustan Times (23 February 2009).
22. The Hindu (7 July 2009).
23. New Kerala (23 February 2009).
24. The Hindu (3 November 2009).
25. *Ambasta Pramathesh, P S Vijay Shankar, and Mihir Shah. (2008). Two Years of NREGA: The Road Ahead. Economic and Political Weekly.*
26. Pinaki Chakraborty (2007). Implementation Employment Guarantee : A Preliminary Appraisal, Economic and Political Weekly,ruary 42 (7), 548-551.
27. Banerjee K and P. Saha. (2010), 'The NREGA, the Maoists and the Developmental Woes of the Indian State', Economic and Political Weekly, Vol. 55, no. 28,pp.42-47.
28. The Times of India (1 April 2012).
29. Centre for Science and Environment. (2008). The National Rural Employment Guarantee Act (NREGA), Opportunities and Challenges, New Delhi, pp 53.
30. The Asian Age (18 July 2011).
31. The Indian Express (8 January 2008).
32. The Hindu (11 October2008).
33. *Ambasta Pramathesh, P S Vijay Shankar, Mihir Shah. (2008). Two Years of NREGA: The Road Ahead. Economic & Political Weekly.*
34. MoRD (2012). "MGNREGA Sameeksha 2012": An Anthology of Research Studies on the Mahatma Gandhi National Rural Employment Guarantee Act (2006–2012) - A Report by the Ministry of Rural Development, GOI.
35. The Financial Express (14 July 2012).
36. The Asian Age (17 June 2007).
37. New Kerala (1 December 2011).
38. Ashok Pankaj, 'Processes, Institutions and Mechanisms of Implementation of NREGA: Impact Assessment of Bihar and Jharkhand', retrieved from http://www.nrega.net/pin/reports-and-resources/reports.
39. Siddhartha & A. Vanaik, (2008). 'CAG Report on NREGA: Fact and Fiction', Economic & Political Weekly, pp.40-45.
40. Parshuram Rai, The Great Job Robbery-Rs 2100 Crore NREGS In Madhya Pradesh.
41. Jean Dreze (20 November 2007). NREGA: Dismantling the Contractor raj: The Hindu.

42. *Jean Dreze, Reetika Khera, & Siddarth. NREGA in Orissa: Ten Loopholes and the Silver Lining" Interim Survey report.*
43. Appraisal of Processes and Procedures of NREGS in Orissa: A study of Mayurbhanj and Balasore District: Department of Humanities and Social Sciences, Indian Institute of Technology, Kharagpur .
44. Retrieved from http://www.downtoearth.org.in/node/2282 searched on 25.1.2013
45 Soumya Mohanty. (2012)." Mahatma Gandhi National Rural Employment Guarantee Act and Tribal Livelihoods: A case Study in Sundargarh District of Odisha" Department of Humanitites and Social Sciences, National Institute of technology, Rourkela.
46. Pradeep Baisakh."MGNREGA performs poorly in poverty stricken Odisha". Retrieved from http://infochangeindia.org/poverty/features/mgnrega-performs-poorly-in-poverty-stricken-orissa.html on 3.2.2013
47. R. Birner, K. Gayathridevi, K.G, Raabe, E. Schiffer, & M. Sekhar (2010). 'How to overcome the governance challenges of implementing MGNREGA', Discussion Paper 00963, International Food Policy Research Institute.
48. R. Jha,S. Bhattacharya, S. R. Gaiha, &S. Shankar (2008). 'Capture of anti-poverty programmes: An analysis of the National Rural Employment Guarantee Programme in India' , ASARC Working Paper 2008/07.
49. Jean Dreze (2007). NREGA: Dismantling the contractor raj: The Hindu, 20th November.
50 . A Roy , J. Dreze & N. Dey. (31 January 2008): 'Finish the Job', Hindustan Times.
51. SRRA (Society for Regional Research and Analysis) (2010). 'Migration of Tribal Women: Its Socioeconomic Effects – An in-depth Study of Chhattisgarh, Jharkhand, M.P. and Orissa', p-89-96.
52. Dreze J, & Oldgies, C.. (2009). 'NREGA implementation countrywide: the first two years'. Frontline.
53. *L. Mathur (2007). Employment guarantee: Progress so far, Economic and Political weekly, 42 (52): 17-20*
54. *G.B. Pant Institute of Social Science (2009): 'Survey of the status of the National Rural Employment Guarantee Act (NREGA) in five sample Gram Panchayat (GPs) of Udaipur Block, Surguja District, Chhattisgarh', pp.1-15, Allahabad.*
55. Jandu N. 2008. "Employment Guarantee and Women's Empowerment in Rural India. Retrived from www.righttofoodindia.org/data/navjyoti08_ employment _guarantee_and_women's_empowerment.pdf.
56. K. Banerjee & P. Saha (2010), 'The NREGA, the Maoists and the Developmental Woes of the Indian State', Economic and Political Weekly, 55, 28: 42-47.
57. CSE (Centre for Science and Environment) (2008). The National Rural Employment Guarantee Act (NREGA), Opportunities and Challenges, New Delhi, p. 53.
58. Khera Reetika & Nandini Nayak (2009). Women Workers and Perceptions of the National Rural Employment Guarantee Act. Economic & Political Weekly, xliv(43).
59. The Hindu (2 January 2009).

60. A. Roy, J. Dreze, N Dey., (31 January 2008): 'Finish the Job', Hindustan Times.
61. One India (15 April 2009).
62. The Pioneer (11 November 2010).
63. Drèze J, and R. Khera.(2009(). "The Battle for Employment Guarantee." Frontline, 26 (1): 3–16.
64. S. Shankar & R. Gaiha (2012). 'Has the NREGS reached the Rural Poor?' Seminar, 629,pp. 68-72.
65. MoRD. (2010). 'Mahatma Gandhi National Rural Employment Guarantee Act 2005: Report to People'. Ministry of Rural Development, GoI, New Delhi.- MoRD (2010). Report of the Working Group on 'Specific Needs of Special Categories under MGNREGA', pp.9-25. retrived from www.nrega.nic.in/CEGC/SpecificNeedsofSpecialCategories.pdf.
66. Siddhartha & A. Vanaik, (2008). 'CAG Report on NREGA: Fact and Fiction', Economic & Political Weekly, p-40-45.
67. The Business Standard (22 August 2012).
68. *Pinaki Chakraborty (17 February 2007). Implementation Employment Guarantee: A Preliminary Appraisal, Economic and Political Weekly42(7): 548-551.*
69. *Ambasta Pramathesh, P S Vijay Shankar, & Mihir Shah. (2008). Two Years of NREGA: The Road Ahead. Economic & Political Weekly*
70. Centre for Science and Environment, 'An Assessment of the National Rural Employment Guarantee Programme in terms of its potential for the Creation of Natural Wealth in India's Villages' www.nrega.net/pin/reports...resources/.../NREGA%20CSE.doc
71. NFIW (National Federation of Indian Women) (2008). 'Socio-Economic Empowerment of Women under National Rural Employment Guarantee Act (NREGA)', pp.-65-76, New Delhi.
72. *Comptroller and Auditor General Report, March 31, 2009.retrieved from http://* /ezinearticles.com/?Labour-Migration:-A-Shadow-of-Poverty-in-Orissa&id=115270, visited 31.1.2013.
73. Jean Dreze (20 November 2007): 'NREGA: Dismantling the Contractor Raj', The Hindu.
74. Institute of Applied Manpower research (IAMR), All –India Report on Evaluation of NREGA: A survey of twenty Districts.
75. *National Federation for Indian Women.(2008). Socio-economic Empowerment of Women under NREGA. retrieved from www.ipc-undp.org/pressroom/files/ipc163.pdf*

Chapter - IV

Ground Realities on Awareness

In a demand driven employment generation scheme such as MGNREGA, the awareness among the people about the important provisions of the scheme is critical for the success of the scheme. Previous research studies reveals that the awareness levels of basic provisions of the Act among rural households were not encouraging. Most available literature on awareness have established that, although it is a well provisioned guideline, there exists a low awareness among the villagers about their rights. The present research study throws new light on awareness levels about MGNREGA in the six states.

Information Source About MGNREGA

Dissemination Of Information is an important function of the State, especially with regard to welfare schemes for the rural population. Ever since the legislations empowering Panchayats in rural areas came into force, it has become the responsibility of Panchayats and other grassroot governance structures to provide the necessary information to the rural population. In the case of MGNREGA, information regarding the employment guarantee scheme has to be given to people by panchayat members or the Panchayat's Notice Board. However, that has not been always the case in most States. The highest proportion of respondents, who got information about MGNREGA from panchayats has been UP at 72.5 per cent. While a majority of respondents in Chhattisgarh, Bihar and Odisha got information about MGNREGA from their respective panchayats, only 32.4 per cent of respondents from Jharkhand got information from panchayats. Interestingly, a majority of 62 per cent of respondents from Jharkhand claimed that the source of information about MGNREGA has been their friends and neighbours. In MP, 32.1 per cent of respondents received information about MGNREGA from media and other sources compared to 41.6 per cent of respondents who got the necessary information from panchayats. These findings reveal that greater emphasis must be given to dissemination of information about MGNREGA at the panchayat level.

Table 14: Sources of information About Mgnrega

Sources	*Bihar*	*Chhattisgarh*	*Jharkhand*	*Madhya Padesh*	*Odisha*	*Uttar Pradesh*
Gram Sabha Members	219(45.6)	287(59.7)	153(31.8)	173(36.0)	265(55.2)	300(62.5)
Gram Sabha Notice Boards	73(15.2)	30(6.3)	3(0.6)	27(5.6)	6(1.3)	48(10.0)
Friends and Neighbors	67(14.0)	96(20.0)	298(62.0)	126(26.3)	159(33.1)	108(22.5)
Media	12(2.5)	22(4.6)	19(4.0)	61(12.7)	3(0.6)	2(0.4)
Other Sources	109(22.8)	59(12.3)	7(1.5)	93(19.4)	47(9.7)	22(4.6)

N: 480

Ignorance keeps the tribals away from benefit of MGNREGA

Mali Behera, *Bayakumutia, Banspal, Keonjhar*

Ms. Mali Behera aged around 42 became widowed and was staying in the village of Bayakumutia of Banspal block of Keonjhar district. Now she lives with her youngest son in the village as two of her older sons (Bishu and Mahato) have migrated out to Chennai. Her other two sons are working on a construction site there, as there is no employment opportunity available in the village. She finds it hard to manage her family due to lack of job opportunity. She manages her family by collecting and selling of firewood from a nearby forest. She claims there is no availability of job under MGNREGA in the locality as per the need and requirement, despite having the job card. Last year she worked for 15 days on the community pond under MGNREGA and got Rs.1000 after two months delay. She doesn't have her passbook so she was paid cash by the GRS. She is completely ignorant of MGNREGA and its provisions, therefore she has never demanded job despite her interest to work in MGNREGA works.

Awareness on Applying For Employment

The process of getting employment under MGNREGA needs to be clear to the people so that they are able to apply for employment under the scheme. Under MGNREGA, each family or household is entitled to job cards that mention the details of all the family members on it. It is only when job cards are prepared, can members of a household apply for employment in MGNREGA work sites. Primary data from all the six states reveal that except for Bihar, where only 11.7 per cent of the respondents were aware of that only job card holders were entitled to employment under MGNREGA, a majority of respondents from other States of the same with Jharkhand having the highest awareness at 62.9 per cent. This finding is an eye opener on the level of awareness of a basic requirement under MGNREGA.

Table 15: Awareness on Who Can Apply For Employment Under Mgnrega

Sources	*Bihar*	*Chhattisgarh*	*Jharkhand*	*Madhya Padesh*	*Odisha*	*Uttar Pradesh*
Job card holder	56 (11.7)	249 (51.9)	302 (62.9)	248 (51.7)	300 (62.5)	282 (58.8)
Any Village member who is above 18 years of age	117 (24.4)	73(15.2)	20 (4.2)	61 (12.7)	39 (8.1)	93 (19.4)
Any one	121 (25.2)	51 (10.6)	56 (11.7)	52 (10.8)	76 (15.8)	47 (9.8)
Do not know	186 (38.8)	107 (22.3)	102 (21.3)	119 (24.8)	65 (13.5)	58 (12.1)

N= 480

Awareness of 100 Days Employment

MGNREGA is a unique scheme which gives legal entitlement for each rural household to get 100 days employment in a year. This right can be accessed by rural households only if they are aware of it. The comparative data on the awareness levels of the rural people in the six concerned States reveal that a significant proportion of respondents are aware of their legal entitlement for 100 days of employment. However the variations between different States are also very large. The rural people of Chhattisgarh appear to be more aware of this entitlement than other States with 73.1 per cent of the respondents aware of this right. A majority of respondents from UP, Odisha and Jharkhand were also aware of the right of 100 days employment. Bihar had the lowest awareness with only 30.2 per cent of the respondents aware of their right to 100 days employment. Interestingly, there are also variations in the levels of awareness of the right of 100 days employment across social groups in different States. In Jharkhand, MP, and Odisha, respondents belonging ST were found to be more aware of this right than other social groups. In UP, respondents belonging to SCs were more aware of this right, while in Chhattisgarh, OBCs were more aware of this right than other communities. In Bihar, in spite of their low awareness levels, it is pertinent to note that SCs and OBCs were more aware of their right to 100 days employment than other communities.

Table 16: Awareness on 100 Days of Work Across The Social Groups

Social Group	*Bihar*	*Chhattisgarh*	*Jharkhand*	*Madhya Padesh*	*Odisha*	*Uttar Pradesh*
Scheduled Tribe	0(0.0)	67(14.0)	152(31.7)	91(19.0)	195(40.6)	9(1.9)
Scheduled Caste	71(14.8)	74(15.4)	89(18.5)	67(14.0)	39(8.1)	294(61.3)
Other Backward Class	69(14.4)	204(42.5)	14(2.9)	47(9.8)	53(11.0)	14(2.9)
General	5(1.0)	6(1.3)	6(1.3)	20(4.2)	0(0.0)	2(0.4)
Others	0(0.0)	0(0.0)	0(0.0)	2(0.4)	0(0.0)	0(0.0)
Total	145 (30.2)	351 (73.1)	261 (54.4)	227(42.3)	287(59.8)	319 (66.5)

N= 480

Ready to work if job under MGNREGA is available in time of need

Giridhari Lakra, *Bogichatola, Kumjharia, Kuarmunda, Sundergarh*

Giridhari Lakra belongs to "Oraon" tribe and lives in Bogichatola village of Kuarmunda Block. He lives with his wife, three daughters and one son. The eldest son is studying in Kumjharia high school and the rest of his two daughters are studying in the village primary school. Last year he didn't get any opportunity to work under MGNREGA, but this year (in January 2012) he has worked in a rural connectivity work for 3 weeks on a daily wage basis of Rs. 125. But he has not been paid his wages for three months. His job card has been taken away by the Gram Sanjojak 3 months ago. He is interested to work under MGNREGA but work is not available as per their need, and delayed payment is a major problem. He has never applied for the job as he is not aware of MGNREGA provisions. He is also unaware of the entitlements as provided under MGNREGA.

Awareness of Different Provisions of MGNREGA

There are different provisions in MGNREGA for which the rural population needs to be aware of for the effective implementation of the scheme. Among them is the provision of unemployment allowance for those who do not get employment within a stipulated period. The awareness of this provision has been very low across all the six States. The highest level of awareness among all the States was found to be from 19.2 per cent of the respondents from Jharkhand. In case any worker gets hurt at the work site, there is provision for accident compensation given to the injured worker. Again the awareness of this provision was found to be very low in all the six States. The highest awareness of accident compensation was found to be in Chhattisgarh, with a rate of 23.4 per cent. The rural people must also be aware of the amount sanctioned and spent for each project so that there is greater transparency and accountability in the implementation of MGNREGA. The awareness levels on allocation are negligible in all the States. A mere 6.9 per cent of respondents each from Bihar and Chhattisgarh were aware of this aspect of MGNREGA, which was higher than other States.

Table 17: Awareness About Provisions in MGNREGA

Provisions	*Bihar*	*Chhattisgarh*	*Jharkhand Pradesh*	*Madhya*	*Odisha*	*Uttar Pradesh*
Unemployment Allowance	15(3.2)	75(15.7)	92(19.2)	56(11.7)	55(11.5)	63(13.2)
Accident Compensation	72(15.0)	112(23.4)	33(6.9)	46(9.6)	27(5.7)	39(8.2)
Amount sanctioned and spent	33(6.9)	33(6.9)	10(2.1)	31(6.5)	23(4.8)	14(0.9)
Gram Panchayat Responsible for Implementation	8(1.7)	270(56.3)	195(40.7)	213(44.4)	179(37.3)	287(59.8)
Gram Panchayat communication updates in the village	60(12.5)	79(16.5)	26(5.5)	64(13.4)	21(4.4)	1(0.2)

N= 480

The MGNREGA empowers the local governance structures to implement its projects and therefore at the village level the Gram Panchayat is responsible for the implementation of various provisions under the Scheme. It is heartening to note that except for Bihar, a large proportion of the rural population is aware of the responsibility of the local Panchayat in the implementation of MGNREGA. A majority of respondents from Chhattisgarh and UP were aware of this aspect of implementation. Similarly more than one-third of the respondents from MP, Jharkhand and Odisha were aware of this provision. It is interesting to note that in spite of the relatively high levels of awareness of the responsibility of Gram Panchayats in the implementation of MGNREGA, there is very low awareness of the communication updates put up by the Gram Panchayats in the village. A comparative analysis of this aspect across all the six States reveal that with 16.5 per cent of its respondents keeping themselves updated with Gram Sabha communication, Chhattisgarh being identified as having the highest number of respondents who are aware of all communication updates from the Gram Panchayat.

The awareness levels of the rural population about various provisions of MGNREGA throws up a mixed picture. While there is a relatively high level of awareness of some provisions of MGNREGA, the level of awareness of other aspects are low. There is a high level of awareness in all the six States of provisions such as the right to 100 days of employment in a year and the need for job cards to get the guaranteed employment. There is very low awareness across all the states on important provisions such as unemployment allowance, accident compensation and the right to know the amount sanctioned and spent for each project. It appears that high levels of illiteracy among the rural masses influence the levels of awareness about MGNREGA. As a result, though rural people are aware of some of the basic features of MGNREGA, they are unaware of the details of the implementation process of MGNREGA.

Chapter - V

Insights into Implementation

Institutional arrangements for the implementation of MGNREGA have been in place in each State with panchayats being engaged in a major way. Consequently, the Department of Panchayat and Rural Development (DPRD) is made the nodal agency overseeing the implementation of MGNREGA in each State. It is responsible for preparing Annual Plans, ensuring that the State receives its share for the implementation of MGNREGA and ensuring smooth flow of funds to the districts. Every State also has a State Employment Guarantee Council that periodically reviews, supervises and monitors the implementation of MGNREGA. It also publicizes it in the widest possible manner and advises the State Government on all matters concerning its implementation. At the District level, the District Programme Coordinator (DPC) consolidates Plan Proposals of Panchayats and prepares a Labour Budget for sanction by the District Panchayat. The Coordinator also coordinates the activities of Programme Officers, review, monitor and supervises MGNREGA works and redress greivances, if any. At the Block level, the Janpad-level Programme Officer matches demand for work with employment opportunities, prepares Block plans, ensures prompt and fair payment of wages as well as allowances and ensures regular social audit, in addition to the normal function of monitoring the projects and addressing complaints. Finally, at the village level, the Gram Panchayat registers households, issues job cards, registers demand for work and allots employment opportunities within 15 days. The picture emerging from this research analysis is far from encouraging.

The rural job guarantee scheme may be floundering with the government admitting the flagship programme suffers from delayed payments, poor awareness, and lack of durable assets, faulty job cards and muster rolls.

Some of the major criticisms of MGNREGA enlisted endemic "lack of awareness about rights and entitlements" and inability of workers' to submit written applications as significant drawbacks. Patchy maintenance of records like job cards, dated receipts and incomplete muster rolls also indicate the scheme is not reaching beneficiaries or is prone to leaks and manipulation. Shortage of dedicated personnel is affecting the task of measuring and certifying completed works. It is also noted that "delay in wage payments and poor coverage of banks and post offices" along with "conduct and quality of social audits" are among major challenges experienced during implementation of the job scheme. More than five years after its rollout - during which it has been hailed for boosting the rural economy and being a buffer against extreme penury - opinion is more divided with calls for recasting the job scheme growing louder and some quarters insisting the programme embodied non-productive expenditure. A major lacuna is that MGNREGA funds are used for works of a non-permanent nature and divert government spending from more productive sectors of the economy is reflected in the ministry's assessment that there is a need to "make assets more durable and productive." Without permanent assets, the money would evaporate.

State governments in general have desisted from paying unemployment allowances to below the poverty level (BPL) job-seekers under the NREGA. At least that was the finding of a national study on the role of Panchayati Raj Institutions (PRIs) in the implementation of NREGA during April to December 2007 by an NGO, PRIA. As much as 68 per cent of the 4,680 households surveyed in 20 districts of 13 States covered by the NREGA had not been provided with a job within the stipulated period of 15 days as specified under the law. The States surveyed were Bihar, Chhattisgarh, Jharkhand, Madhya Pradesh, Odisha, and Uttar Pradesh. The reason was these States were unwilling to dole out the money. Secondly, such payments reflected poorly on the performance of the state and the officials concerned, who could invite penal action (The Hindu, 2008)[1]

Thus, the main problems in implementation of MGNREGS are definition of a household, denial of registration, delay in distribution of job cards, fees being charged for work application forms, non-issuance of receipts, absence of worksite facilities, non-availability of muster rolls at worksite, shortage of staff, delay in appointments, non-availability of regular works, delay in wage payment and payment less than the minimum wage (Kohli, 2009).

Job Cards

One of the formalities which are essential for getting employment under MGNREGA is the making of a job card. Each family has one job card with details of the family and bank account in it.

> ***Villagers don't need Job Card due to less payment and delay in payment***
>
> ***Village / GP – Chandaka, Block-Pottangi, District-Koraput***
>
> *The Scheduled Caste village of Chandaka of Pottangi block has 49 households all belonging to SC community and the population was around 207. All the households in the village were found to be equally poor. Their survival and sustenance depended on daily wage work. Many of them revealed that lack of work availability forced them to migrate to Andhra Pradesh, which is around 150 km away from the village to work there as a daily wage labourer. The village level verification found that out of the total households, 14 families (i.e., 35 per cent of families) did not possess job cards and seems to be less interested to get the job card. The reason for not seeking job cards was the delay in payment of wages, which sometimes extends for many months. In addition, they also said that the wages they receive under MGNREGA was little compared to the amount of work they do. Yet, they revealed that they earn more outside the State (the daily wage rate in Andhra Pradesh was Rs 200- , whereas MGNREGA pays Rs. 125 per day). Therefore, the scheme did not attract them to apply for the job card. When the findings were brought into the notice of Panchayat Officials, the officials tried to defend themselves by saying that those families often migrate out, therefore job cards was not issued in their names. Those who do not migrate are having the job cards. Those officials perhaps have forgotten that MGNREGA was designed with many objectives including the objective to check migration. Therefore, the migrant families should be issued the job cards on a priority basis rather than other families.*

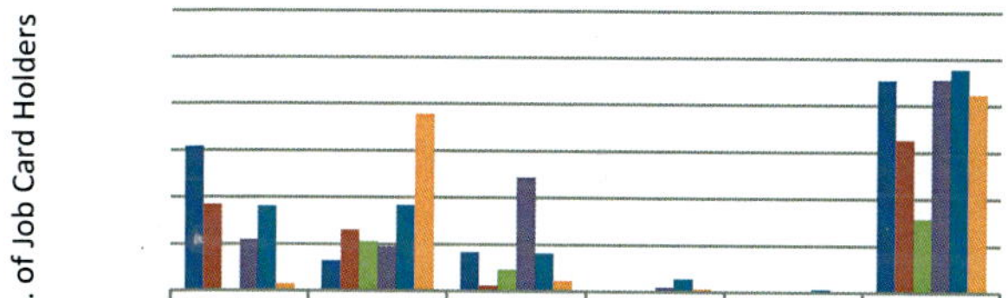

	ST	SC	OBC	General	Other	Total
Odisha	308	64	83	0	0	455
Jharkhand	184	130	12	0	0	326
Bihar	2	106	47	3	0	158
Chattisgarh	109	94	243	10	0	456
Madhya Pradesh	181	183	81	27	6	478
Uttar Pradesh	15	379	23	7	0	424

Figure 1: Job Card Holders (N= 480 per State)

Job cards are issued by the Gram Panchayat to the applicants free of cost within a month after application is made. The primary data on job cards reveal a mixed picture in the six States. While an impressive 99.6 per cent of the respondents in Madhya Pradesh had job cards, only 32.9 per cent of the respondents in Bihar were job card holders. Chhattisgarh, Odisha and UP showed hopeful signs with around 90 per cent of the respondents having job cards, but the implementation of MGNREGA in Jharkhand is a matter of concern as nearly one-third of the respondents not having job cards. However, a large number of job card holders are from the socio-economically backward communities such as STs, SCs and OBCs.

MGNREGA still eludes poor and needy in Koraput

Arjun Bisai, Nuagaon (Majhi Sahi), Haldikunda, Boipariguda, Koraput

At the age of 30 years Arjun Bisai, has to look after his eight-member family. Apart from his widowed mother, his wife, four sons and one daughter mostly depend on him and his income. Arjun who belongs to "Sundhi" tribe of Nuagaon village lost his father Late Kamal Lochan Bisai almost 20 years back. The family has one acre of rain fed land which is not sufficient to manage a large family. Arjun and his wife go for wage employment in the village for additional income. They are also engaged in the collection and selling of minor forest produce that fetch them some income during the year. One day, the Ward Member told him about "MGNREGA" and its provision of 100 days job guarantee in 2007. So he applied and got a job card by paying Rs.10 to the ward member. But no work under MGNREGA has been provided to Arjun Bisai till date. He is not alone when it comes to not getting jobs under MGNREGA.

False entry in Job Card

Mahana Singh, Kaladihi, Kaptipada, Mayurbhanj

Mahana Singh belongs to "Kulla" tribe of Kaladihi village. Mahana is illiterate and owns a small patch of agricultural land. He has seven members in his family with four daughters. His elder daughter was assisting him in agricultural activities and often goes out to do agricultural labour. As the small land holding did not maintain a seven member family, he along with his wife and daughter also go for wage employment in the village and nearby areas. Only once during last year he had worked for nearly two weeks in a farm pond under MGNREGA and earned Rs.1500. As per Mahana, he had never demanded job under MGNREGA, but the job card verification found that he had applied three times for job; it was dated 3.05.08 for 100 days, on 19.02.09 for 50 days and on 29.07.09 for 30 days. On the other hand as per the record in the Job Card he had received Rs.2400 for the same work. Apart from this, his job card was showing that he had received payment of Rs. 945 and Rs.2400, which he never received. He also revealed that his ration card is taken away by somebody since last 3 months and as a result he is not getting even PDS items.

Job cards of poor tribals are taken away by the Sarpanch

Budra Padhi, Mariguda, Petturu, Pottangi, Koraput

Paraja tribe is one of the most backward tribal communities in Odisha. Whether it is education, social and economic development, they are found to be lagging behind on all socio-economic indicators. Budra Padhi is a resident of the Mariguda Village, belonging to Paraja Tribe. The six member family, including three sons and one daughter, is found to be landless. Their major source of livelihood is daily wage labour. As the employment opportunity is limited in their village, they mostly depend on agricultural labour. As getting agricultural work is limited to agricultural session only, they find it hard to manage the large family. The family has been registered under MGNREGA and had received the Job Card during the year 2006. But it is taken away by the former Sarapanch of Petturu GP and till date it has not been returned. He doesn't know about the purpose of the job card and its benefits. He also doesn't have a ration card at present and so he is not getting benefits under PDS and other social welfare schemes of the government.

All job cards have expired

Districts - Hardoi Sitapur, Azamgarh and Allahabad.

A very common issue found at all four districts is that almost all MGNREGS Job cards had expired for the last 2-3 years in every district. There no application that has been found forwarded for a new job card by the Gram Panchayat at block level, so the job cards holders were left with no other option other than still use the same job card for getting employment under MGNREGS. They were also unaware about the expiry of their job cards for the last 2-3 years. In Azamgarh district, one year ago, the Gram Pradhan sent a request for a new job card, but yet as of 24/09/12 no job card updating request has been accepted. Even the Pradhan continues to be in touch with his requisition, but still the application remains under process.

Job card of SC community taken away by Gram Pradhan

Allahabad district, Kaudihar block, Bamrauli Uparhar Panchayat

Mr. Chhuggan Lal is a resident of the Bamrauli Uparhar Panchayat, Kaudihar Block, Allahabad district. The main source of livelihood for his family was daily wage labor work. He has six members in the family including 2 sons and two daughters. Mr. Chhuggan was registered under MGNREGS in 2006. From the start of MGNREGA, Mr. Chhuggan has kept his job card from the period of (2006-2010).But after the recent Gram Panchayat election, the current Pradhan not only kept his job card but also that of the whole SC community. Here a very interesting thing is that the Pradhan is also belonging to his community. Mr. Chhuggan has many times requested Gram Pradhan to release his job card but he did not receive it. Even he didn't know about the hidden agenda of the Pradhan and the importance of job cards. He was only aware that the job card is used for identity proof like a ration card, which is provided by the Government to only MGNREGS labor, and he has the authority to keep it. This invited corruption in the MGNREGS work.

Though it has been heartening to note that job cards have been provided to a large number of rural households, the process of making job cards has not been as smooth as it should have been. Normally, job cards should be provided less than a month after the household completes registration for a job card. Primary data from the six States reveal that with the exception of UP, where 73.1 per cent of the respondents admitted that they received job cards within a month after registering for it, in all other States less than half the respondents received their job cards in less than a month. Bihar has fared very poorly with only five per cent of respondents receiving job cards within a month. In other cases, it took upto five months and even more to Receive Their Job Cards.

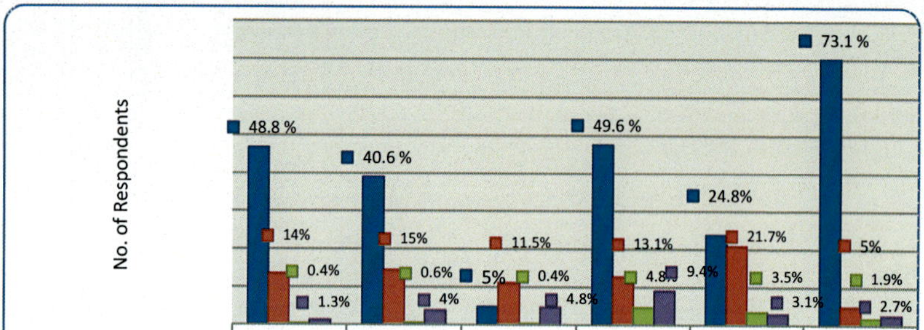

	Odisha	Jharkhand	Bihar	CG	MP	UP
Within one month	234	195	24	238	119	351
2-3 Months	67	72	55	63	104	24
3-5 Months	2	3	2	23	17	9
More than 5 months	6	19	23	45	15	13

Figure 2: Receipt of Job Card After Registration (N= 480 per State)

Information whether job cards are issued free of cost, the highest percentage of positive trend was observed in Odisha (90.4 per cent); and lowest of 18 per cent was noted in Bihar. While an equal of nearly 61 per Cent Was Noted In The State of Jharkhand And Uttar Pradesh.

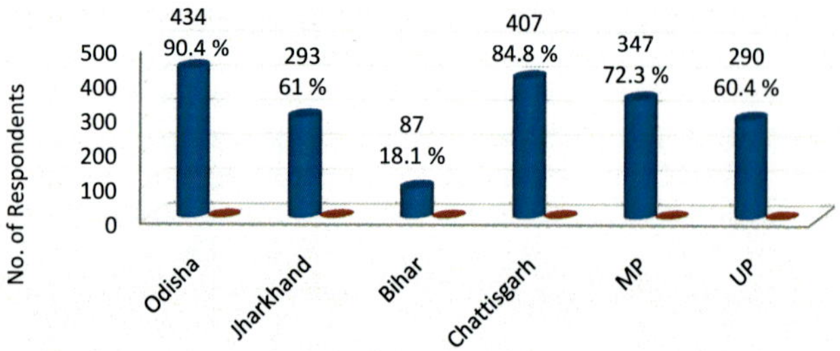

Figure 3: Job Card Issued Free of Cost (N= 480 Per State)

Decision Making for Project Selection

With regard to participation in Gram Sabha for the purpose of decision making for selection of projects, an overall 19 per cent respondents out of 2880 (480 each from the six states) 548 together reported that they were involved in decision-making process for selection of projects in Gram Sabha. A comparative analysis of this across all the six states reveal that a highest proportion of positive responses on the same were 156 from Chhattisgarh and the lowest level was 24 in Bihar. Odisha (101) and Jharkhand (112) showed somewhat involvement level in decision making process for selection of projects in Gram Sabha.

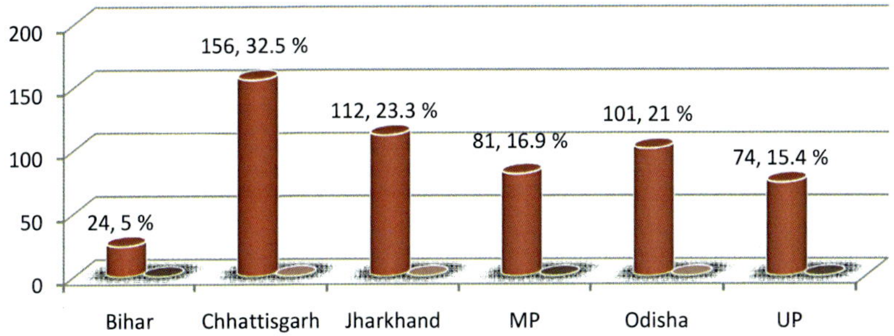

Figure 4: No. And Percentage Of Respondents Involved In Decision Making For Project Selection In Gram Sabha

Time Taken for Employment

Within 15 days of submitting the application or from the day work is demanded, employment is provided to the applicant. The primary data from all the 2880 respondents from all the six states indicate 1135 respondents who were provided with employment under MGNREGA within 30 days after submitting application. Out of this a highest proportion of 87 per cent respondents were from UP, 63 per cent respondents were from Jharkhand, 27 per cent respondents were from MP, 22 per cent respondents were from Chhattisgarh, and a lowest proportion of 19 per cent respondents were from Bihar and Odisha respectively estimated from 480 respondents from each of the six states equally.

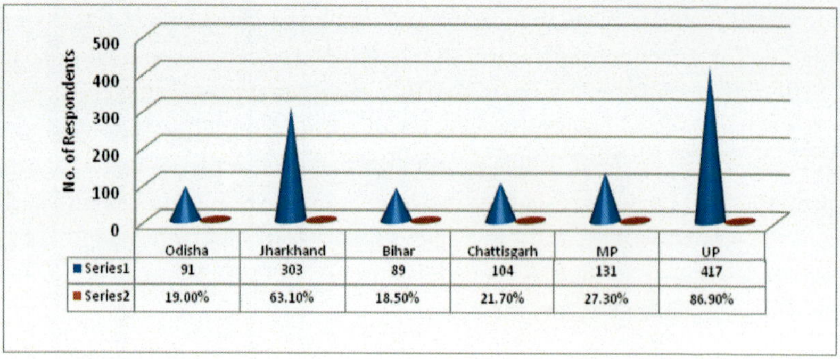

Figure 5: Within 30 Days Taken to Give Employment Under Mgnregs After Applying N=480

Wage Rate and Work Days

The wage rate paid under MGNREGAwas much lower than what had been prescribed under the Minimum Wages Act. States have the freedom to fix minimum wages. The job act as a law that "guarantees those at the bottom of the economic pyramid their basic entitlements" and the payment of minimum wages under the act had "created a synergy" between the MGNREGA and the wage act (The Telegraph, 2012).[2]

100 Days Employment

One of the key provisions of MGNREGA is that it provided at least one hundred days of guaranteed wage paid public employment in a financial year to every household whose adult members volunteer to engage in unskilled manual labour. This right for 100 days wage employment hoped to address the problem of unemployment and under-employment in rural India. However, primary data from the six States reveal that a very small percentage of people got at least 100 days of wage employment. With 6.8 per cent of respondents getting at least 100 days of employment, MP had the best performance compared to all the other States. A large majority of respondents in almost all the States got employment for less than 50 days. In Chhattisgarh, 55 of the respondents got less than 25 days of employment during the last one year. This clearly indicates that a lot more needs to be done to ensure that rural households get their full entitlement of 100 days employment guaranteed under MGNREGA.

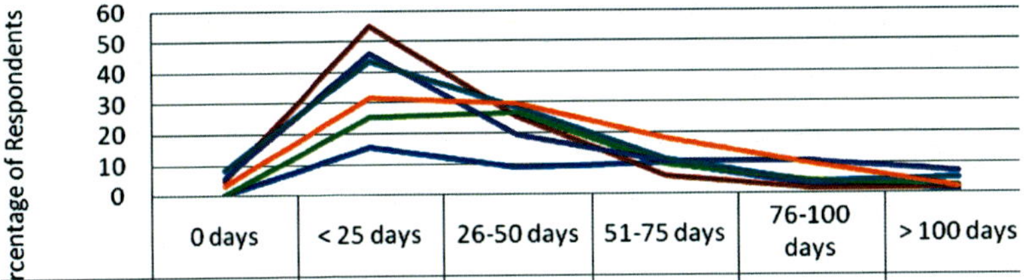

	0 days	< 25 days	26-50 days	51-75 days	76-100 days	> 100 days
Bihar	0	15.4	8.6	10	2.5	0.8
Chhattisgarh	4.6	55	25.2	5.6	1.2	1.4
Jharkhand	0	25.2	26.5	9.6	3.8	2.2
MP	5.6	45.8	19.2	10.4	10.4	6.8
Odisha	8.1	43.5	28.1	11.2	3.3	4.7
UP	3.2	31.6	29.5	17.8	9.3	1.8

Figure 6: Employment Days

> ***Irregularity of employment leads to discrimination among the beneficiaries***
>
> ***Allahabad district, Koraun Block, Belhat Panchayat***
>
> *Mr. Brijbhan is a resident Manglapuri Hamlet, Belhat Panchayat, Koraun Block of Allahabad district, and his main source of income is agricultural and daily wage labour. Despite MGNREGS provision of 100 days full employment opportunity to rural people at the household level, here the case is different. Mr. Brijbhan claims that there is irregularity of employment under this Act, which is causing discrimination among the beneficiaries. He claims that MGNREGS could not provide work continuously. So for earning a living we have to go to the other side of our place where we can earn money. Most of the time we are engaging in pre-decided work, so we do not get the opportunity to work continuously. This is the biggest reason for dividing the beneficiaries. For instance, if MGNREGS work begins on Monday 10/12/12, we are relieved on Thursday 13/12/12, and hence, this creates discrimination in terms of number of employment days.*

Unemployment Allowance

In case the person does not report for work within 15 days of being notified by the Gram Panchayat or Programme Officer, he/she would not be entitled for the Unemployment Allowance. However, the effect of employment not given to any eligible applicant within 15 days of his/her demanding work or the date from which he/she sought work by way of submitting application, should lead to provision of Unemployment allowance according to the laid down MGNREGA guidelines. On an overall basis, the primary data reveals that just 48 respondents out of a total 2880 respondents covering all the six states together received Unemployment

Allowance. A highest proportion of just three per cent respondents each from Chhattisgarh and MP (out of 480 respondents per state) reported the receipt of Unemployment Allowance. As per the norms, the rate of Unemployment Allowance should be one-fourth of the wage rate for the first 30 days and half of the wage rate afterwards during that particular financial year which is again subject to the household entitlements of days of employment.

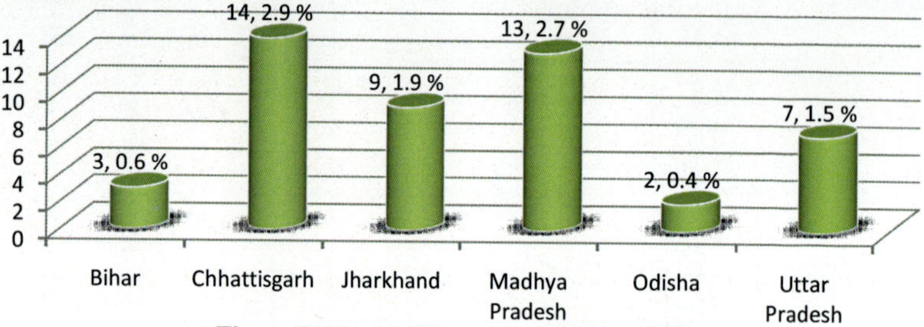

Figure 7: No. and Percentage of Respondents Who Received Unemployment Allowance

Information Source About MGNREGA Works

Overall, the proportion of respondents among 2880 total respondents from all the six states under study, who received information about the works allotted under MGNREGS cover and its availability from Gram sabha notice board were 4 per cent (138); Gram sabha members were 35 per cent (1008); friends-neighbours were 33 per cent (939) and Munadi 7 per cent (211). Further, a comparative state-wise analysis showed a highest proportion of nearly 8 per cent each in Chhattisgarh and Madhya Pradesh from Gram sabha notice board, 39 per cent each in Odisha and Madhya Pradesh with Gram sabha members as information source out of 480 respondent households from each state. Bihar accorded a lowest proportion of 14 per cent for Gram sabha members, and merely 1 per cent for Gram sabha notice board as source of information regarding works allotted and its availability.

Table18: Source Of Information About The Works Allotted And Availability

	Gram Sabha Notice Board		*Gram Sabha Members*		*Friends/Neighbours, Others*		*Munadi*	
	No	%	No	%	No%	No	%	
Bihar	4	.8	70	14.6	21	4.4	0	0
Chhattisgarh	42	8.8	109	22.7	110	22.9	208	43.3
Jharkhand	12	2.5	77	16.0	234	48.8	0	0
MP	40	8.3	187	39.0	245	51.0	2	.4
Odisha	8	1.7	189	39.4	277	57.7	1	.2
UP	32	6.7	376	78.3	52	10.8	0	0

N=480

Distance of Worksite

The MGNREGA guidelines notifies that if a person applies, the work needs to be provided within 5 km of the beneficiary's residence. In case the work is provided beyond five km radius of the residence then the beneficiary is entitled for 10 per cent additional wages towards transport and living expenses. Overall, a high proportion of 2165 out of 2880 respondents from all the six states stated that worksite was within 5 kms from their respective villages. Comparative state-wise analysis revealed a highly positive response in this regard, where Odisha, Madhya Pradesh, Uttar Pradesh, Chhattisgarh, Jharkhand accorded 93.1 per cent, 91.9 per cent, 90.6 per cent, 81.9 per cent, and 66.5 per cent respectively out of 480 respondents from each state.

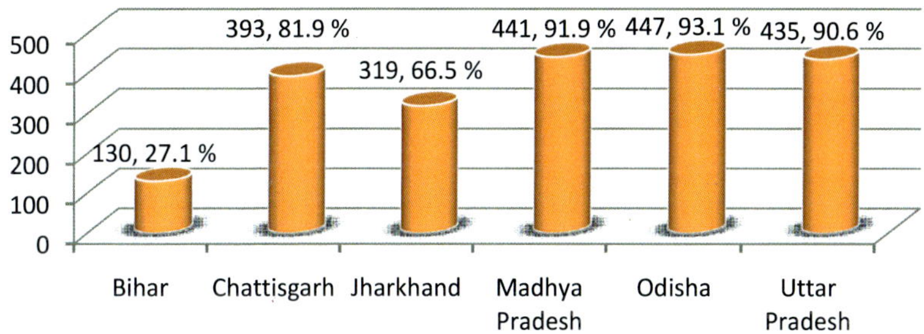

Figure 7: No. & Percent Of Respondents With Work Site Within 5 Km From Village

Not getting compensation despite given job more than 5 kms away

Jathu Behera (JC No – 24402), Bayakumutia, Banspal, Keonjhar

Jathu Behera is a resident of Bayakumutia village in Keonjhar district. He belongs to "Bhuyan" tribe. Last year he worked 15 days in Kaipur village under

MGNREGA, which is more than five km away from his village. He had to bear his own expenses to get to the worksite. Earlier he was told that he will be paid for the extra cost of travel but he was not paid for it. He had worked for Rs 70 on a daily wage basis and had received of Rs.1050/- from that work only.

Worksite Facilities

As per MGNREGA guidelines there is a provision of facilities for its workers, with regard to safe drinking water, period of rest, first aid, and crèche facility at the MGNREGS work site. Overall, out of 2880 total respondents from all the six states under study taken together, a highest proportion of 1464 respondents were provided with safe drinking water, 1147 respondents were provided with period of rest, 447 respondents were provided with first-aid facility, and nearly 64 respondents were provided with crèche facility. A state-wise comparative analysis showed out of 480 households, a maximum of 439 (91.5 per cent), 305 (63.5 per cent), and 164 (34.2 per cent) respondents from Chhattisgarh enjoyed worksite facilities of safe drinking water, period of rest, and first-aid respectively. The state of Bihar performed poorly in terms of safe drinking water (5.6 per cent) and first-aid box (1.3 per cent).

Table 19: Facilities at Work Site

	Drinking Water		*Rest Period*		*First Aid*		*Creche*	
	No.	%	No.	%	No.	%	No.	%
Bihar	27	5.6	118	24.6	6	1.3	-	-
Chattisgarh	439	91.5	305	63.5	164	34.2	9	1.9
Jharkhand	304	63.3	284	59.2	127	26.5	14	2.9
MP	315	65.6	230	47.9	108	22.5	40	8.3
Odisha	208	43.3	63	13.1	1	0.2	1	0.2
UP	171	35.6	147	30.6	41	8.5	-	-

N=480

Satisfaction Level On Working Conditions Under MGNREGA

Information was gathered to understand the level of satisfaction with regard to the working conditions provided under MGNREGS. Overall out of 2880 total respondents, 273 were highly satisfied, 1104 were moderately satisfied, while 729 were not satisfied at all on the same. Comparative state-wise analysis with 480 respondents from each of the six states, a highest proportion of 66.9 per cent from Chhattisgarh, 49.6 per cent from Odisha, 42.9 per cent from Uttar Pradesh, 32 per cent to 36 per cent from Jharkhand and Madhya Pradesh, and a lowest of 3 per cent from Bihar were moderately satisfied with the working conditions and the facilities provided at the worksite. A highest proportion of 114 respondents from Uttar Pradesh stated to be highly satisfied, while a highest proportion of 181 respondents from Jharkhand were not satisfied at all with the prevailing working conditions provided under MGNREGA.

Table 20: Satisfaction Level On Working Conditions Provided Under MGNREGS

	Highly Satisfied		*Moderately Satisfied*		*Not Sure*		*Not Satisfied*	
	No.	%	No.	%	No.	%	No.	%
Bihar	14	2.9	15	3.1	410	85.4	41	8.5
Chhattisgarh	54	11.3	321	66.9	31	6.5	74	15.4
Jharkhand	7	1.5	152	31.7	140	29.2	181	37.7
Madhya Pradesh	41	8.5	172	35.8	117	24.4	150	31.3
Odisha	43	9.0	238	49.6	43	9.0	156	32.5
Uttar Pradesh	114	23.8	206	42.9	33	6.9	127	26.5

N=480

MGNREGA benefits still eludes the tribals

Kamlung Mundagadia, Nuagaon, Haladikund, Boipariguda, Koraput

Kamlung Mundagadia belongs to "Gadaba" tribe and lives with his wife and children in Nuagan Village of Koraput district. He is a poor and marginal farmer with 1.5 acres of non irrigated land. He finds it hard to arrange sufficient food and other basic requirements for his family. So the couple goes for daily wage labour. He claims that he has been working under MGNREGS for the last two years. Works under MGNREGS is not provided as per his requirement and demand. And always the payment is delayed and it is very hard for a poor family like his to wait for wages, when they live on a daily basis. Realizing his need and family condition, Gram Rozgar Sewak and others suggested to him to apply for land development under MGNREGS. He applied accordingly as per norms in May 2011 in the Gram Panchayat Office, but to his dismay the application was rejected. He said that work was given to another person in his village.

Wage Payment and Process

One of the important guidelines of MGNREGA is that the wages need to be paid every week, or in any case not beyond a fortnight after the date on which such works are done under its cover. However, a proportion of the wages in cash may be paid on a daily basis. The present study found an overall 509 respondents out of a total 2880 respondents who received payment on a weekly basis. Comparative analysis based on 480 respondents from each of the six states, revealed a highest of 38.5 per cent from UP, 30.4 per cent from MP, 17.7 per cent from Jharkhand, 8.1 per cent from

Odisha and lowest proportion of 5.6 per cent each from Bihar and Chhattisgarh who received payment for their works done on a weekly basis.

Table 21: Payment Done for Work

	Daily		*Weekly*		*Monthly*		*More Than One Month*		*Not Sure*	
	No	%	No	%	No	%	No	%	No	%
Bihar	10	2.1	27	5.6	61	12.7	0	0	382	79.6
Chhattisgarh	6	1.3	27	5.6	140	29.2	186	38.8	121	25.2
Jharkhand	2 .	4	85	17.7	161	33.5	0	0	232	48.3
MP	11	2.3	146	30.4	112	23.3	0	0	211	44.0
Odisha	6	1.3	39	8.1	234	48.8	0	0	201	41.9
UP	4	.8	185	38.5	222	46.3	0	0	69	14.4

N=480

Muster rolls needs to be available and maintained at the worksite. Every worker should be entitled to check the muster roll at any time. It is a record of attendance of labour every day either by own self or through the mate in the prescribed Muster Rolls at the worksite. With respect to the process adopted for payment of wages, an overall 1325 respondents out of a total 2880 respondents from all the six states revealed that Mustar Rolls were followed and to ensure timely payment of MGNREGS wage labour and when Mustar Rolls were not followed as a payment process. When a comparative state-wise analysis was done, an encouraging response was observed with 84.6 per cent and 60 per cent in UP and Jharkhand respectively (out of 480 respondents per state). However, MP (46 per cent), Chhattisgarh (40 per cent) and Odisha (36 per cent) also showed a somewhat satisfactory trend in this regard.

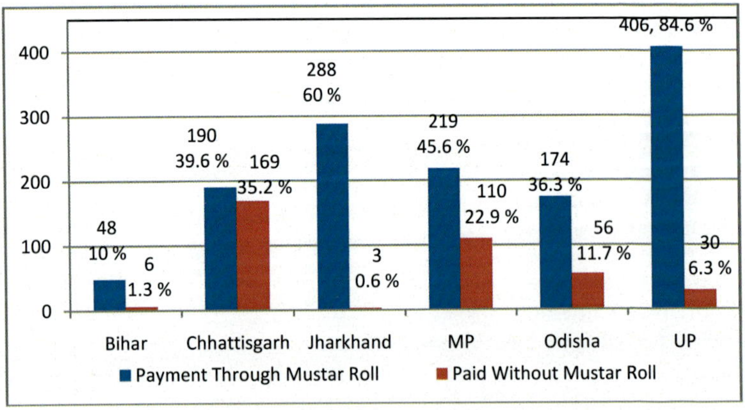

Figure 9: No. and Percentage of Respondents for Process for Payment

Delayed payment under farm pond is found to be common

Haribandhu Majhi, Goudaguda, Boipariguda, Koraput

Haribandhu Majhi belongs to "Bhumia" tribes, resides in the village Gaudaguda of Boipariguda GP / Block of Koraput district. He was a small marginal farmer with two acres of land. Due to lack of irrigation facility the agricultural production was not sufficient to feed his family. Thus, both wife and husband prefer to work as casual labour including MGNREGS work. As per the suggestions of a Ward Member, he applied for a farm pond under MGNREGS and got work order on 20/05/2010. Excited over the allotment he took extra interest and completed all works within the stipulated period (20 days) by engaging around 20 workers from his village. All the workers engaged were not having Job Cards so he spent Rs.1000 to get the Job Cards of all 20 beneficiaries as per the instruction of a well known contractor of the area. He was quite happy initially but it did not last. The estimated cost of the project was Rs.50,000, but after five months of the completion of the work he could only get Rs.22, 000. After years he is still waiting for the rest of his amount of Rs.28, 000. He is still unsure whether his due payment would be made or not.

Nonpayment still haunt communities

Balaji Harijan, Ranaguda, Ramgiri, Boipariguda, Koraput

Balaji Harijan, SC by caste is a resident of Ranaguda village, Ramagiri GP of Boipariguda block of Koraput district. Agriculture has been the major source of livelihood for the family. The 4 acres of non-irrigated agricultural land seldom meet the yearly family expenses, so they go for wage employment whenever they find it. He applied for a farm pond under MGNREGS in 2011 and got the work order (letter no- C/R-No-21-2010-11). He remembers the work was completed within 22 days by employing 17 villagers. After three months of completion of the work, he was paid Rs.27, 000, when the estimated cost of the farm pond was Rs.50, 000. The rest of the amount of Rs 23,000 has not been paid till date, despite repeated reminders and running behind the implementing officials.

Despite delay and nonpayment MGNREGA still brings hope

Budra Gollari, Ranaguda, Ramgiri, Boipariguda, Koraput

Budra Gollari belongs to "Rana" caste which is considered to be OBC in Odisha. He lives with his seven members' family in the village of Ranaguda of Ramgiri GP under Boipariguda block of Koraput district. For the family, agriculture is the main source of livelihood, but that is always not enough to sustain the large family. So the adult members goes for wage employment in the village. According to Budra, MGNREGS could be a boon for the working poor. He was visibly happy when he counted that his family had earned Rs. 7000 from MGNREGS work during the year 2011. He worked in coffee plantation work carried out by Soil-Conservation Department. But all is not well for him. He got a farm pond in 2010 with an estimated cost of Rs. 50,000. He remembers that it took 14 labourers to complete the work in 25 days. After three months of completion of the work he was paid only Rs. 27,000 by cash. For release of the rest amount he has been unsuccessfully running to the Panchayat officials and the concerned JE of Boipariguda Block. He is told that the rest of the amount has not been sanctioned and it might take a few more months. Despite all the bad experiences, he has not lost hope on MGNREGA. He says things are not so bad in 2011. He has a greater satisfaction with this scheme, as his farm pond has proved to increase his agricultural production manifold. With some assured irrigation he is now growing vegetables like cauliflower, lady's finger, tomato etc. He assumes that during the year2012, the production would further increase compared to the previous year.

Monitoring and Overseeing of MGNREGS Works

Overall, 793 respondents out of a total 2880 respondents from all the six states shared that a Monitoring Committee was set-up for works at the village level. A comparative state-wise analysis (480 respondents per state) on the same showed that a proportion of 44 per cent respondents from UP, nearly 36 per cent respondents each from Jharkhand and Chhattisgarh, 28 per cent respondents from Odisha and a smallest proportion of six per cent respondents from Bihar stated that such monitoring committee was set-up for works at the village level.

Further, a highest proportion of 28 per cent respondents from Chhattisgarh, nearly seven per cent respondents each from Jharkhand and MP, nearly 4 per cent respondents from Odisha, and just a single respondent from Bihar stated that this monitoring committee presents its report to the Gram Sabha.

Besides identification of eligible household for registration under MGNREGA, Gram Rozgar Sevak (GRS) should assist in the verification of the registered households. The GRS along with mates are responsible for distribution of wage payment slips amongst workers. An overall 1453 respondents out of a total 2880 respondents from all the six states informed that a GRS was appointed for looking after MGNREGS works. The primary data based on a comparative state-wise analysis (out of 480 respondents per state) showed a highest proportion of 83 per cent respondents from Odisha, nearly 72 per cent respondents each from Chhattisgarh and Uttar Pradesh, 54 per cent respondents from Jharkhand, and a low proportion of 15 per cent to 8 per cent respondents from MP and Bihar reported on the same information. It is apparent that both the number and quality of human resources deployed so far are completely inadequate for carrying out the multifarious responsibilities under MGNREGA implementation.

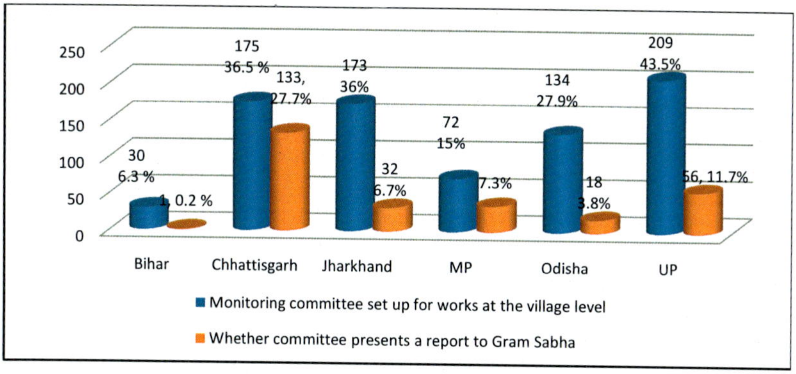

Figure 10: Monitoring of Mgnregs Works N=480 Per State.

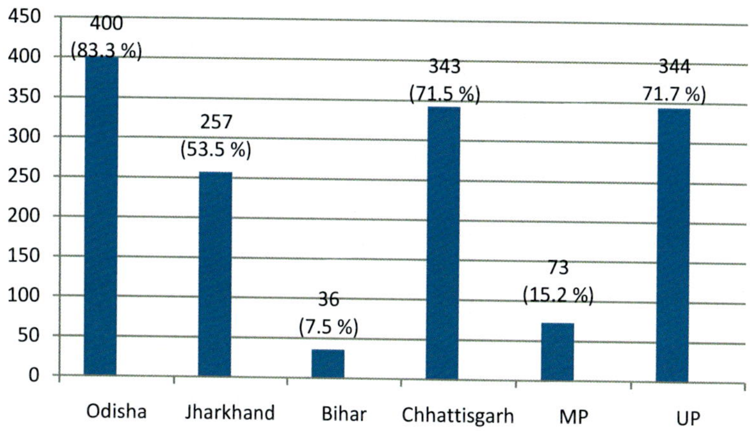

Figure 11: Gram Rozgar Sevak for Mgnrega.

Information on monitoring and overseeing of MGNREGS projects in process revealed that out of a total 2880 respondents from all the six states, 614 informed that gram sabha members were involved on the same, 380 respondents informed that Mukhia was involved, 325 informed that Panchayat President was involved, while 227 respondents informed about the involvement of Block Officials in the overseeing of MGNREGS projects in process. A comparative state-wise analysis (out of 480 respondents per state) reflected a highest proportion of 68 per cent respondents from UP where Gram Sabha members were involved, 40 per cent respondents from Chhattisgarh where Panchayat President were involved,31per cent respondents from MP where Mukhia was involved, and 28 per cent respondents from Odisha where Block Officials were involved in monitoring and overseeing of project works in process under MGNREGA. Both in case of Jharkhand (19 per cent) and Bihar (13 per cent) Mukhia played an important role in overseeing of MGNREGA project works in process in their respective areas.

Table 22: Monitoring and Overseeing of Projects in Process

	Gram Sabha members		*Panchayat President*		*Mukhiya*		*Block officials*		*Others*	
	No	%	No	%	No	%	No	%	No	%
Odisha	66	13.8	42	8.8	22	4.6	136	28.3	51	10.6
Jharkhand	11	2.3	2	0.4	91	19.0	71	14.8	65	13.5
Bihar	14	2.9			60	12.5			11	2.3
Chhattisgarh	146	30.4	191	39.8	20	4.2	13	2.7	6	1.3
MP	50	10.4	65	13.5	148	30.8	3	.6	122	25.4
UP	327	68.1	25	5.2	59	12.3	4	.8	5	1.0

N=480

Irregularity often dissuades the potential beneficiaries

Dasrath Singh, Pital, Chitapedi, Sundergarh

Dasarath Singh is a landless resident of Pital village of Chitapedi Gram Panchayat of Nuagaon Block of Sundergarh district. He belongs to Rautia caste considered to be from OBC. He and his family solely depend on daily wage employment for their survival. Last year he worked under MGNREGA in piece rate basis and lifted around 70 "chauka" and per chauka rate was fixed at Rs.163. Hence he should have received around Rs.11040. But after six months of the completion of the work he was paid only Rs.8370. The rest of the amount is not yet paid. He has already written a complaint to the concerned BDO, but there is no response. His eldest daughter Jayanti Singh is now 20 years old, but her name is not mentioned in the Job card for which she is not allowed to work under MGNREGA.

Lost hope due to erratic behavior of implementing officials

Ram Tigga, Rainchapal, Kumjharia, Sundergarh

Ram Tigga belongs to "Oraon" tribe and lives in Gunjhatola hamlet of Raichhapal village of Kumjharia Gram Panchayat of Kuarmunda Block of Sundergarh district. The three member family (including wife and nephew) owns around 4 acres of land, and they are mostly engaged in agriculture for their living. Last year in the month of February a farm pond under MGNREGS was approved to him with an estimated budget of Rs.50,000. He engaged around 10 local labourers for the work for one month and he had to stop the work after that as per instruction of the Junior Engineer (JE). The payment was done after one month interval and surprisingly only Rs.11,000 was released against the sanctioned budget. He was told that he could not complete the work in stipulated time therefore the money has returned back to the head office located in New Delhi. He is completely unhappy over the matter and says that he had applied as per the instruction given by former Sarpanch of Kumjharia. In the process, the Gram Rozgar Sevak (GRS) has taken away his job card for the last one year and has not returned it.

If you don't work under MGNREGA your BPL card would be ceased

Anandamasi Lagoon (JC No - 14723), Pital, Chitapedi Nuagaon, Sundergarh

Anandamasi Lagoon, aged around 50 years now lives with his second wife and three daughters (Asha Lagoon, studying in class 7, Sarita Lagoon studying in class 3 in Gadibaru residential school and his youngest daughter is in class 1 in a local school) in Pital village of Chitapedi GP. His two sons (Manoj 15 years, Premdan, 13 years) dropped out from school after completing class six and have now migrated to Surat (Gujarat) and are working as labourers in some factory. His first wife died due to complication during the delivery of their child. Anandamasi has two daughters (Bardani Lagoon, 21 years of age and Rilan Lagoon 18 years of age) from his first wife. Both his daughters are now in Delhi, working as maid servants in some "Seth" (rich man)'s house. Anandamasi Lagoon produces rice and pulses in his one acre of land. Apart from this he also does tailoring in the nearby market, which fetches him around Rs.1000 a month. He has got the Job Card under MGNREGA and also a BPL card. Around one and half years back the GP officials said that if anyone does not work under MGNREGA his/her BPL card would be seized by the government. Fearing his BPL card would be seized, Anandamasi joined the work under MGNREGA. He dug soil for one month to save his BPL card. As he does not have Bank Account, he borrowed some account from a fellow villager and handed it over to GP officials. They kept it for two months and said this would not work. Since then he has been running from pillar to post to get his wages but has failed to get it.

Notes

1. The Hindu (2008). October 11.
2. The Telegraph (2012). January 22.

Chapter - VI

Impact on the Poor

There is extensive literature demonstrating the importance of MGNREGA in India's rural development. These studies can be mainly categorized in two different segments: firstly, the potential of NREGA, which includes quite a significant number of literature that are mainly based on the massive potential of the reforms suggested in NREGA. Most of these studies have examined the operational efficiencies of the NREGA. Secondly, the impact on rural households, wherein, the academicians and policy makers have also taken increased interest in assessing the impact of MGNREGA on the rural households from different aspects, namely, awareness, impact on the livelihoods, women empowerment, rural-urban migration, agricultural wages, marginalized sections, implementation problems, and so on.

There have been many evaluation studies on the impact of NREGA on women. Based on field data derived from 1060 of NREGA workers from states of North India, Khera and Nayak (2009)[1] studied the socio-economic consequences of NREGA for women. They observed that though there were drawbacks in Bihar, Chhattisgarh, Jharkhand, Madhya Pradesh, Rajasthan and Uttar Pradesh in implementation of the NREGA, it has started providing significant benefits to rural women by offering access to local employment at the statutory minimum wage with relatively decent and safe work conditions mostly in their own village. Taking different case studies, the study also observed that NREGA has helped in improving gender relations in some of the most remote areas of the country. Similarly, the impact of NREGA on women empowerment in four northern Indian states revealed a direct impact of NREGA in increasing the social status of women. The study revealed that NREGA had benefited rural women in two ways: first, it has opened a new avenue of paid employment; and, second, it has broadened their choices and capabilities, by reducing dependence on other family members. It was also revealed that MGNREGA can also have a significant positive impact on reduction in child labour through income effects and women's wellbeing and empowerment. According to the study, the programme had increased income through higher wage rates, rise in agricultural wages, decline in migration, and so on.

These positive effects can in turn reduce child labour and increase the participation of children in education. The less privileged communities in India have also benefited from NREGA. A state wise analysis of the Act shows that, compared to the share of population in India of SCs and STs, the participation rates in NREGA have been much higher in almost all states. Similarly, NREGA, by guaranteeing employment, has also alleviated the problem of rural-urban migration. It is assumed that it has impacted both the seasonal and the permanent migration trends. Seasonal migrations were reduced because rural workers secured employment during the lean season at their home districts. Permanent migrations are also likely to have been be reduced because of rural development (Drèze et, al, 2008).[2]

Apart from its contribution to households, NREGA has had a beneficial impact on the community and village economy. Drèze et.al. 2007 found that 92 per cent of workers felt that the NREGA work was useful and 83 per cent felt that NREGA has led to useful assets creation. Most of these studies showed that the coverage of NREGA at the micro-level, i.e. at the panchayat level and village levels, has varied within the country. In other words, the Act has varied impact across states.

The MGNREGA employment trends validate the hypothesis that it is the neediest who seek employment under the Scheme. In a survey conducted in 2008 in Bihar, Chhattisgarh, Jharkhand, MP, and UP—it was found that a majority of the MGNREGA workers belong to the most disadvantaged sections of society; 81 per cent of the sample workers lived in kachcha (non-permanent) houses, 61 per cent were illiterate, and 72 per cent have had no electricity at home. SC and ST families accounted for 73 per cent of the workers in the randomly selected sample.

Therefore, MGNREGA has had an impact in rural India in different ways. The findings of the primary data on six States, namely Bihar, Chhattisgarh, Jharkhand, MP, Odisha and UP attempts to assess the impact of MGNREGA on income, education, agriculture, women and the functioning of PRIs in its implementation of the programme.

Impact on Household Income

The main feature of MGNREGA is that it provides guaranteed wage employment for 100 days, thus enhancing household income. A comparative study of the six States reveal that a significant proportion of the rural population do feel that the implementation of MGNREGA has increased household incomes. State-wise variations have been within a tight range from 52.1 per cent of the respondents from Odisha expressing this view to 22.3 per cent of respondents from Jharkhand sharing this view. It is pertinent to note that the majority of the respondents in all States barring Odisha did not subscribe to the view that MGNREGA has increased household incomes. The study also reveals that rural people do experience that MGNREGA has been a source of assured income for the household though there are huge State-wise variations. On the one hand, over 70 per cent of the respondents from Uttar Pradesh claimed that MGNREGA has been a source of assured income for them; on the other hand, only 8.1 per cent of the respondents in Jharkhand expressed the same view. The opinions in other States varied from 15.4 per cent in Bihar to 37.5 per cent in MP. This finding should spur greater efforts to ensure 100 days of employment to the rural population and even consider increasing the number of days of guaranteed employment in rural areas to ensure that MGNREGA increases rural household incomes and that it is a source of assured income for improving rural livelihoods.

Table 23: Assured and Increased Income.

States	*Assured Income*	*Increased Income*
Bihar	74 (15.4)	113 (23.5)
Chhattisgarh	122 (25.4)	148 (30.8)
Jharkhand	39 (8.1)	107 (22.3)
Madhya Pradesh	180 (37.5)	196 (40.8)
Odisha	136 (28.3)	250 (52.1)
Uttar Pradesh	339 (70.6)	234 (48.8)

N=480

A positive perception of the rural poor, that MGNREGA is economically beneficial to them, is crucial for the effectiveness of the flagship programme. Primary data on the perception of the rural population of the six States regarding the economic benefits of MGNREGA reveal that barring Bihar and Jharkhand, a majority of the respondents in the other States perceive MGNREGA as economically beneficial to them, though the intensity of their perceptions differ widely. In Bihar only 11.5 per cent of the respondents perceived that MGNREGA has been economically beneficial in some way or the other while in Jharkhand 58.1 per cent of the respondents categorically stated that MGNREGA has not helped them economically at all. Among the States with a more positive perception about MGNREGA, Odisha tops with 82.4 per cent of the respondents admitting that MGNREGA has been economically beneficial to them. However, in Uttar Pradesh, where 82 per cent of the respondents had positive perceptions of MGNREGA, the intensity of their perceptions were much greater compared to other States with 8.1 per cent of the respondents saying that MGNREGA has been highly beneficial and 42.9 per cent of them admitting that MGNREGA has been moderately beneficial.

Table 24: Perception that MGNREGS has Helped Economically

Perception	*Bihar*	*Chhattisgarh*	*Jharkhand*	*Madhya Pradesh*	*Odisha*	*Uttar Pradesh*
Very Much	20(4.2)	25(5.2)	3(0.6)	7(1.5)	35(7.3)	39(8.1)
Moderately	13(2.7)	153(31.9)	54(11.3)	198(41.3)	186(38.8)	206(42.9)
Little	22(4.6)	126(26.3)	144(30.0)	157(32.7)	174(36.3)	149(31.0)
Not at all	213(44.4)	166(34.6)	279(58.1)	108(22.5)	83(17.3)	74(15.4)
Not Sure	212(44.2)	10(2.1)	0(0.0)	9(1.9)	2(0.4)	12(2.5)

N=480

One of the secondary effects of MGNREGA is that since the wage for MGNREGA was fixed at Rs. 100 per day and above, it led to an increase in rural wage rates for casual labour for men and women and this in turn has also led to an increase in household incomes. Primary data from all the States have confirmed the trend of rising rural wages in 2012 compared to that of the preceding year. This is consistent with the findings of the Planning Commission and NSSO that the introduction of MGNREGA has led to an increase in rural wage rates, which in turn results in an increase in household incomes. Increase in household incomes also has other secondary effects as increase in purchasing power and disposable incomes that could be used for creating productive assets and investing in human capital of rural households.

Table 25: Mean Daily Wage Rate in 2011 & 2012 for Men and Women

States	*Men*		*Women*	
	2011	2012	2011	2012
Bihar	122.08	134.93	26.53	86.86
Chhattisgarh	83.62	89.69	69.25	75.18
Jharkhand	110.77	129.94	73.82	92.42
Madhya Pradesh	110.58	134.87	94.74	111.78
Odisha	74.66	77.98	61.61	64.56
Uttar Pradesh	105.36	121.79	92.38	106.52

N=480

Farm pond is adding to the household income

Raghunath Murch, Nuagaon, Haldikunda, Boipariguda, Koraput

Ragunath Murch aged around 35 years, belongs to Gadaba tribe. There are five dependent members in his family. He applied for a Farm Pond in April 2011 and got it with an estimated cost of Rs.50,000. The work was completed within 20 days, but he received Rs.43,000 in February 2012. When he enquired about the less payment both the bank official as well as the Panchayat officials said that this is what the total amount is. Despite not getting the entire amount he seems to be happy as the farm pond is adding to his income by providing irrigation and fish.

Despite some odds MGNREGA has increased household income by creating assets

Krishna Pradhani , Nuagaon, Haladikund, Boipariguda, Koraput

Krishna Pradhani lives with his wife and three children (one son and two daughters) in the village Nuagaon of Boipariguda block. The family belongs to "Rana" caste which is considered to be OBC. They have a small agricultural land holding, which is not sufficient to sustain the five member family, so the couple goes for wage employment. In 2011 he applied for a farm pond under MGNREGA, which was subsequently sanctioned with an estimated budget of Rs. 50,000. After five months of the completion of the work only Rs. 45,000/- was sanctioned against the estimated cost, through the Bank (Utkal Gramya Bank, Ramgiri Branch). But he finally received Rs. 40,000 and the rest of the amount of Rs.5000 has not been paid yet. Krishna had to borrow Rs.3000 from his relatives to meet the labour payment. To add to his problems, the wage amount of one beneficiary was deposited in the other's account, due to confusion of account number. He had to struggle to pursue with the beneficiary to return the amount to the actual beneficiary. Despite all odds, Krishna has started fishery from this year. He is hopeful that by next year the fish production would increase and he could make a good living out of fishery. To him MGNREGA support is quite critical but it is not hassle free and full of problems.

Impact on Employment

One of the main objectives of MGNREGA has been to generate employment opportunities in rural areas in order to reduce rural unemployment and under-employment. In spite of the inefficiencies in the implementation of MGNREGA, to a large extent the rural population has benefitted in terms of employment. The MGNREGA was found to be popular among people living in rural areas of India, in particular the concerned six States, for three main reasons: (1) It provided for employment during lean season; (2) It provided for easy availability of employment within their own gram panchayat; and (3) It provided for employment for women with wage equal to men. The capacity of MGNREGA to generate employment in rural areas was found to be more popular in UP than in other States. In spite of India's fast growing working population, the potential of MGNREGA to help the country come close to full employment is immense.

Table 26: Impact of MGNREGA on Employment

States	*Employment during Lean Season*	*Easy Availability of employment*	*Employment of Female Member*
Bihar	84 (17.5)	116 (24.2)	69 (14.4)
Chhattisgarh	228 (47.5)	211 (44.0)	379 (79.0)
Jharkhand	85 (17.7)	25 (5.2)	80 (16.7)
Madhya Pradesh	198 (41.3)	143 (29.7)	244 (50.8)
Odisha	226 (47.1)	200 (41.7)	433 (90.2)
Uttar Pradesh	267 (55.6)	331 (69.0)	359 (74.8)

N=480

One of the important objectives of MGNREGA has been to prevent distress migration of people from rural areas to urban centres. Primary data from the six States confirm that some beneficiaries of MGNREGA have stopped migrating to other places in search of work on account of the availability of work in their own villages, though there are huge State-wise variations in this trend. From among all the States, a majority of respondents (52.1 per cent) from Uttar Pradesh have stopped migrating in search of employment elsewhere. Half of the respondents from Odisha shared this trend. However, only 11.9 per cent of the respondents from Bihar and 13.1 per cent of respondent from Jharkhand have said that they have stopped migrating on account of MGNREGA. Interestingly, the land holding status of those who have stopped migrating to other urban centres reveal that in all the States, it is largely landless people and small farmers who have stopped migrating in search of work.

Sold out domestic cows to pay the MGNREGA wage

Budhiram Marandi, Kaladihi, Kaptipada, Mayurbhanj

Budhiram Marandi a tribal belongs to "Santhal" community is living in Daraga Sahi of Kaladahi village under Kaptipada Block. Agriculture has been a major source of income for the family. He was enthused when he got a farm pond in his name under MGNREGA, as this was going to add to the asset of the family and would fetch some additional income. The project that was sanctioned during 2009-10 had an estimated cost of Rs.35,000. He engaged 20 villagers to work in the farm pond and completed the work in one and half months time. After 3 months of the completion of the work the payment was made and to his surprise only Rs.20000 was credited as against the estimated budget. He was told that the remaining amount has gone back and that he would not be paid because the estimated work didn't match the work done. Hence he was forced to sell his cows to pay more than Rs.5000 additional labour cost to the villagers who had worked in his farm pond.

Farm pond has become a debt trap for Doitari in Mayurbhanj

Doitari Mahato, Tombahora, Pithagola, Badasahi, Mayurbhanj

Doitari Mahato, OBC by caste, is a resident of Tombahora village of Badasahi block. The family has three acres of rain fed agricultural land. The land holding agriculture has been a loss making venture due to erratic rainfall and non availability of irrigation facility. Last year he applied for a farm pond under MGNREGS, which was approved in the Palli Sabha. Despite the approval from the Gram Sabha he could not get the work order, on the other hand he was asked to pay Rs.1700 to the local Panchayat Executive Officer (PEO) / VLW for getting the work order, which he obliged. After paying the money the Village Level Worker (VLW) asked him to start the work, which he did with the hope that payment would be made. He employed 50 villagers to complete the farm pond within 20 days. But the payment has not been made and he had to sell his household belongings to pay for the wages of labourers. In this way he has spent around Rs.34000 from his pocket. He is now completely in a debt trap and there is no sign of payment from government. Looking at the miserable condition of the family, his two sons now have dropped out of their education and migrated out to Kerala to bring the family out from the debt trap. The farm pond has been a debt trap for the family and has totally shaken the family socially and economically.

Table 27: Land Holding Status Of Households Who Have Stopped Migration

Land Holding	*Bihar*	*Chhattisgarh*	*Jharkhand*	*Madhya Pradesh*	*Odisha*	*Uttar Pradesh*
Landless	43(9.0)	136(28.3)	23(4.8)	83(17.3)	49(10.2)	94(19.6)
<2 acres	11(2.3)	49(10.2)	32(6.7)	23(4.8)	98(20.4)	115(24.0)
2-4 acres	1(0.2)	12(2.5)	5(1.0)	8(1.7)	64(13.3)	29(6.0)
4-10 acres	2(0.4)	6(1.3)	2(0.2)	5(1.0)	29(6.0)	12(2.5)
>10 acres	0(0.0)	1(0.2)	1(0.2)	1(0.2)	0(0.0)	1(0.2)
TOTAL	57(11.9)	204(42.5)	63(13.1)	120(25.0)	240(50.0)	251(52.3)

N=480

Impact on Agriculture

A lot of emphasis of MGNREGA has been on water and soil conservation, building check dams, wells and other assets in order to improve the productivity of agriculture especially of small and marginal farmers in rural areas. Primary data from the six States reveal that there are differing opinions on whether agricultural output in rural farms has increased on account of MGNREGA. On the one hand, 61.5 per cent of the respondents from Odisha claimed that agricultural output in village farms have increased on account of drought proofing works as well as soil and water conservation works conducted as part of MGNREGA, on the other hand, only 1.3 per cent of the respondents from Jharkhand share this view. There has also been a perception of a negative fallout of MGNREGA on agriculture on account of attribution of a perceived shortage of agricultural labour to MGNREGA works. This perception has been widely rejected in all the States except in Uttar Pradesh, where 45.8 per cent of the respondents shared this view.

Table 28: Impact On Agriculture

States	*Better Agricultural Output*	*Agricultural Activity Affected due to Insufficient Labour*
Bihar	38 (7.9)	71 (14.8)
Chhattisgarh	152 (31.7)	85 (17.7)
Jharkhand	6 (1.3)	13 (2.7)
Madhya Pradesh	152 (31.6)	70 (14.5)
Odisha	295 (61.5)	29 (6.0)
Uttar Pradesh	189 (39.4)	220 (45.8)

N=480

Impact on Women

The encouragement for the participation of women in MGNREGA works has created some impact in the gender relations in rural areas. Except for Bihar and Jharkhand, a large majority of the respondents from the rest of the States have overwhelmingly endorsed the view that the implementation of MGNREGA has made a significant difference in the lives of women and have contributed to their empowerment in rural India. A large majority of respondents in the States of Chhattisgarh, Madhya Pradesh, Odisha and Uttar Pradesh have strongly acknowledged that there has been a lot of emphasis given to the participation of women in works related to MGNREGA.

Table 29: Impact on Women

States	*Women's Contribution improve Household livelihood*	*Encouraged women's Participation in MGNREGA works*	*Improved women's status in household*	*Improved women's status in village*
Bihar	48 (10.0)	29 (6.0)	40 (8.3)	20 (4.2)
Chhattisgarh	417 (86.9)	412 (85.8)	400 (83.3)	211 (44.0)
Jharkhand	122 (25.4)	95 (19.8)	57 (11.9)	10 (2.1)
Madhya Pradesh	386 (80.4)	401 (83.5)	300 (62.5)	169 (35.2)
Odisha	422 (87.9)	409 (85.2)	351 (73.1)	266 (55.4)
Uttar Pradesh	386 (80.4)2	370 (77.1)	375 (78.1)	351 (73.1)

N=480

The availability of employment for women under MGNREGA and the equal wages for men and women has also led to the perception among a vast majority of over 80 per cent of the households in the four States that women make a significant contribution to household income, which has led to the improvement of livelihoods of rural households. In a country where the gender disparity is very high, primary data indicate that there is a strong perception that MGNREGA improved the status of women in a majority of households in the four States as they are contributing to augment household's livelihood. However, fewer respondents were willing to concede that the introduction of MGNREGA has led to the improvement in the social status of women at the village level.

MGNREGS reduced female migration

Hardoi district, Sursa block, Hardoi gramin Panchayat, Mannapurwa Hamlet

Ms. Devaki, is resident of Mannapurwa hamlet of Hardoi Gramin GP, Sursa block, in Hardoi district. Her main source of livelihood is daily wage agricultural work. She is also working as a non-agricultural daily wage worker far from the village. Earlier, she and her husband had migrated from the village to a local market. Ms. Devaki believes that MGNREGS really helped especially in the reduction of women's migration and also the promotion of female employment at the village level. Before the commencement of MGNREGS, the rate of female migration in her village was more than it is now. In recent times, MGNREGS has increased the opportunities for women.

MGNREGA is a hope for tribal widow

Pyari Bhengra, Beldipa, Kuarmunda, Sundergarh

Pyari Bhengra, a tribal (Munda) widow, lives with her two daughters and one son in Beldipa hamlet of Kuarmunda Block, after her husband's death in 2008. Her husband died in the Andamans, when he was there as migrant labourer. Now she is the only earning member in the family to sustain four members. She is landless, so she solely depends on daily wage employment for her survival. When work is available outside the village, she does not mind to go out to earn a living. Last year, one of her daughter, Kunima, passed 10th class but due to financial problem she could not give her further education. Now she is taking tailoring training in the village. She is very much interested to work under MGNREGA but the work is not available as per the need. She has never received more than one month of work under MGNREGA. Last year she had worked 15 days and earned Rs.1500.

Forced to migrate leaving behind the family to suffer

Mini Behara, Patrapur, Badasahi, Mayurbhanj

Ms. Mini Behera manages her family consisting of three children (two daughters and one son) in the absence of her migrating husband Ratikant Behera. Mini who belongs to "Bitiya" caste of SC community lives in Patrapur village of Mayurbhanj district. Her eldest son is studying in class 2 and the other two children are below five years of old. The family is landless and hence they solely depend on daily wage labour to survive. Her husband Ratikant has migrated to Jaleswar, Sikharpur to work in a brick kiln as there is no employment available in the village. He visits his family once in every three months and stays with his wife and children for three to four days during each visit. Mini says her husband is not interested to work outside leaving behind his family in this condition, but there is no alternative available in the village. She is not aware on MGNREGA and its provisions. Therefore she has never demanded a job under MGNREGA. She is also completely unaware about the process of application. She remembers, last year she got three weeks work in the community pond in the village which fetched her Rs.1500. She was paid in cash by one gentleman, who took her thumb impression in one paper and withdrew money from the Patrapur Baitarini Gramya Bank. She says the family job card and bank account (pass book) has been taken away by Gram Rozgar Sevak (GRS) around three months back and it has not been returned to her.

Gift of MGNREGA: Rashmita is now going to college, courtesy MGNREGA

Padal Siniyas, Baraja, Chandaka, Pottangi, Koraput

Padal Siniyas aged 46 years belongs to Nukuda Dora caste (OBC) and lives in Baraja village. As he is landless, the three member family has to depend on wage labour. As wage employment opportunity in the village was limited, he along with the family members often migrate to Andhra Pradesh for their survival. In this process, his daughter Rashmita at the age of 12 years in 2005, while studying in the 5th standard dropped out of school. Padal has completed 100 days of work in the current financial year. Before implementation of MGNREGA, he was migrating to Andhra Pradesh with his entire family. Once there was a meeting about MGNREGA scheme in the village near the house of Padal Siniyas. He attended the meeting and came to know about the rules and provisions of MGNREGA. After two days he applied for a job card with the help of a ward member on 28th of May 2006. He got the card within a week and soon he was called for work under MGNREGA scheme. He and his wife worked for 14 days at that time and received Rs.980. When he saw the amount, he decided not to go out in search of work. As he collected the money, he decided to give education to his daughter. So he went to the school and asked the head master about his daughter re-joining in the school again, in the same class. The head master accepted his request and his daughter continued to go to school. Now she has passed 10th standard from Pattangi Govt. High school and joined the Koraput College. Padal Siniyas is now very happy looking at the progress of his daughter. He said, "MGNREGA scheme has changed my living and it gives me a happy and beautiful life; Thanks a lot to MGNREGA".

Birasmoni works under MGNREGA to pursue her graduation

Jagdish Bhakta, Pital, Chitapedi, Sundergarh

Jagdish Bhakta lives in Pital village of Chitapedi GP with his wife and two children. His two elder sons have been married and are staying with their own families separately. The family has got some agricultural land and agriculture has been their main source of livelihood. Due to uncertainty and less income from agriculture, he prefers to work as a daily wage labourer. His younger daughter Birasmoni is pursuing her graduation at Bisra College of Rourkela. The family income from agriculture is not enough to meet all the needs, including the education expenses of Birasmoni. Therefore, she also engaged herself in daily wage employment under MGNREGA with the aim to earn money for her own study. Last year she worked in a road project with her mother and earned Rs.10200. Jagdish says, that income helped a lot for her daughter's education as she could purchase her books and rest amount she has saved in the local bank for her study purpose. That amount also helps her as she regularly commutes to the college by bus. The only problem was that the payment was made after six months of work. "It was a long wait ", Jagdish said.

Impact on PRIs

MGNREGA presumes that local governance structures function in a way that benefits local communities in rural areas. Primary data reveals that rural people are not satisfied with the performance of their local governing agencies in the implementation of MGNREGA. The comparative study of all the six States reveals that the perception of the performance of Panchayati Raj Institutions (PRIs) is very low. The highest approval of the performance of PRIs among the six States has been from 39.8 percent of respondents from Chhattisgarh and the lowest approval of the performance of PRIs came from Bihar at 0.6 percent.

Table 30: Perception that Pris Are Playing An Important Role in Implementation of Mgnrega

States	*PRIs playing important role*	*PRIs not playing its role*	*Not Sure*
Bihar	3 (0.6)	1 (0.2)	476 (99.2)
Chhattisgarh	191 (39.8)	107 (22.3)	182 (37.9)
Jharkhand	12 (2.5)	255 (53.1)	213 (44.4)
Madhya Pradesh	137 (28.5)	178 (37.0)	165 (34.4)
Odisha	44 (9.2)	105 (21.9)	331 (69.0)
Uttar Pradesh	159 (33.1)	217 (45.2)	104 (21.7)

N=480

Popularity of MGNREGA

There have been reports that the popularity of MGNREGA has been declining over the years and the initial enthusiasm in the implementation of MGNREGA has diminished. Primary data from all the six concerned States reveal that with the exception of Bihar, MGNREGA is hugely popular in other States where respondents prefer that this employment guarantee scheme should continue. In UP as many as 97.7 per cent of the respondents favoured the continuation of MGNREGA. With just over one-third of the respondents preferring the continuance of MGNREGA, Bihar was the only State where MGNREGA was not popular. However, what is most significant is that in all the States, it was the landless and the small farmers who have overwhelmingly supported the continuance of MGNREGA in their respective villages.

Table 31: State-wise Land Holding Status of Respondents Favouring Continuity of Mgnrega

Land Holding	*Bihar*	*Chhattisgarh*	*Jharkhand*	*Madhya Pradesh*	*Odisha*	*Uttar Pradesh*
Landless	132 (27.5)	280 (58.3)	94 (19.6)	308 (64.2)	125 (26.0)	229 (47.7)
<2 acres	24 (5.0)	87 (18.1)	186 (38.8)	68 (14.2)	205 (42.7)	189 (39.4)
2-4 acres	3 (0.6)	32 (6.7)	43 (9.0)	27 (5.6)	93 (19.4)	32 (6.7)
4-10 acres	5 (1.0)	10 (2.1)	9 (1.9)	12 (2.5)	33 (6.9)	17 (3.5)
>10 acres	2 (0.4)	4 (0.8)	3 (0.6)	0 (0.0)	0 (0.0)	1 (0.2)
Not Sure	0 (0.0)	0 (0.0)	0 (0.0)	0 (0.0)	0 (0.0)	1 (0.2)
TOTAL	166 (34.6)	413 (86.0)	335 (69.8)	418 (87.1)	456 (95.0)	469 (97.7)

N=480

Daughter got married without incurring any debt

Nirmal Barla, Teliposi, Kuarmunda, Sundergarh

Nirmal Barla aged 47 years is Christian by religion and belongs to the "Munda" tribe. He lives in Teliposi village with his wife Nayami, two sons and three daughters. Now two of his elder daughters got married and are staying with their husbands. Last year, he got his second daughter Sabita married in Purnapani village of Nuagaon Gram Panchayat. He has got 2.5 acre of agricultural land, but the income from agriculture is not sufficient to maintain his family. He works as a daily wage labourer to add to his income. Last year he got Rs.7000 from MGNREGA work. He got this amount in three phases from the post office at Kuarmunda. He was happy to receive that amount as that helped him for his daughter's marriage. He did not borrow any money for the marriage ceremony and could purchase assets like box, cupboard and utensils from the MGNREGA wage money. Recently, he had applied for his land development in the Gram Panchayat under MGNREGA. But his application was not approved by the Gram Sabha. Anyway he is happy that MGNREGA helped him get his daughter married.

The comparative analysis of the impact of MGNREGA in the six States reveals that in spite of all the flaws and inefficiencies in the implementation of this employment guarantee scheme, it has made quite an impact in rural India. MGNREGA has resulted in augmenting household incomes directly as well as indirectly on account of increased rural wage rates. It has increased the availability of employment in rural areas which has curbed rural-urban migration to some extent. It has also empowered women by providing them equal wages on par with men. In spite of the inefficiencies in the implementation of MGNREGA and the disappointment of rural people with the performance of PRIs in their villages, MGNREGA continues to be very popular with the rural masses.

Thank you MGNREGA

Tularam Nayak, Kuladiguda, Sasahandi, Boriguma, Koraput

Tularam Nayak aged 45 years belongs to "Gadaba" tribe. He has 4 acres of non-irrigated land in his village Kuladiguda. Due to erratic rain and without irrigation the land was almost unproductive. He came to know from a Ward member in March, 2010 about the 'Farm Pond' scheme. After getting information from him, he applied for a farm pond. Within 15 days he got the work order and the work began on April 2010 and he completed the farm pond by June 2010. Now he is cultivating vegetables like egg plants, okra, beans, spinach, peanuts, tomato etc. He said with smile that MGNREGA scheme is going to change my economic life. He exclaimed "Thank you MGNREGA scheme". Due to the farm pond he is now self employed for 5 to 6 months in a year.

Notes

1. Khera Reetika & Nandini Nayak. (2009).Women Workers and Perceptions of the National Rural Employment Guarantee Act. Economic & Political Weekly, xliv (43).
2. A.Roy., J Dreze & N Dey (31 January 2008): 'Finish the Job', Hindustan Times.

Chapter - VII

Solutions Towards Improving the Effectiveness

Many in India argue that the MGNREGA is one of the most important parts of socio-economic legislation passed in recent times. However, the emphasis in our recommendations lies on key features that could significantly contribute to strengthening implementation and accountability relationships in MGNREGA.

Need for Large Scale Awareness Campaign

Experiences on implementation of MGNREGA so far shows that although the rural households are familiar with the name of the scheme and its basic guarantee of 100 days of employment, however, most of the workers or potential workers do not know that the payment of wages is based on the work done. Also there is a weak awareness around the issues of demand for work or provision of social audits.

Specific communication strategy needs to be evolved which should focus on specific messages which enhance guarantee for employment and promote transparency and accountability. Engagement of Civil Society Organizations could help the state in increasing the awareness on various provisions.

Simplifying Job Card Process

- Overall nearly 18 per cent households are without job cards and many of them are willing to work under MGNREGA. The process of card preparation has been stopped or deferred for some reason. It was informed by many poor households that due to lack of job card or due to lose of the card, they have to hire card from other families agreeing for lower wage payments. In this regard, it is good to bring MGNREGA card preparation under Service Guarantee Act so that within a fixed time any one applying for job card is guaranteed to get it.

Ray of hope for a destitute

Shubadra Golari, Nuagaon, Haldikunda, Boipariguda, Koraput

Shubadra Golari, lost her husband almost ten years back when she was only 40 years old. After the death of her husband, she had to struggle to sustain her three member family, including two sons. Shubadra is now 50 and living with her younger son who is 17 years old. Her eldest son is married and is living separately with his family in the village itself. She heard one day from the ward member about "MGNREGA" and 100 days of guaranteed work. Then she applied for a job card which she got within one month. Recently, she worked for 20 days in a farm pond and got Rs.1500 as wage. According to her this scheme is good for the poor like her for their survival.

Promoting Demand for Work by Efficient Management of Payment

There is a decrease in demand for MGNREGA work across all the states as workers are finding it economically unviable to work under MGNREGA. There is a low measurement of work to adjust work of many dormant workers. Moreover, overall only 18 per cent beneficiaries received payment on a weekly basis and the average delay in payments is more than 3 to 4 weeks. Therefore, opportunity cost of working for MGNREGA is very high. The poorest of the poor have high cash crunch for daily living and high vulnerability due to insufficient food security. Therefore, it is imperative that MGNREGA workers get payments within 15 days to keep them engaged in MGNREGA. In this regard, the following need to be considered:

- Strong monitoring at the district level on the muster roll and payment gap analysis to identify villages having delayed payments.
- Ensure that the workers endorse their signature/thumbprint on the muster roll daily; and that muster rolls are available for public scrutiny at worksite.
- Ensure proper maintenance of muster rolls; that they are serially numbered for the entire block, incorporating the block code; that they are entered online, and are thus available publicly.
- Increased availability of civil engineers for verification of muster rolls and work measurement. In certain districts where there is an

acute shortage of civil engineers, a panel of professionals or retired civil engineers can be identified. These empanelled civil engineers can be hired for by the Panchayats for verification of records and measurements.

Village Panchayats should be supported in preparing participatory annual plans and effective labour budgeting so that the most deserving cardholders may get maximum number of employment days.

Promoting Engagement of Gram Sabha for Effective Accountability and Transparency

Gram Sabha is the most important institution for demanding accountability and transparency from the implementing agencies. It is found that Sarpanch and Panchayat Secretary are the key sources of information or information providers. They have weak knowledge and awareness on social audit and complaint register. Similarly, Gram Sabha is not actively engaged in undertaking annual planning. In this regard, the following need to be considered:

- Large scale awareness campaign with Gram Sabhas need to be organized in collaboration with local NGOs to understand their role in social audits. In each block or district, a person should be appointed/ assigned to review the social audit reports and asked for feedback on its non-compliance.
- Gram Sabha actually is not held to conduct social audits. So, a random check of the social audits by the civil society organization/ review agencies needs to be done for identifying the quality of processes and participation of the workers in social audit.
- It is essential to have mentors for facilitating the social audit process. The mentors can be active educated youth from the village or civil society representatives. The state will have to ensure that these mentors are adequately oriented and capacitated so that they are able to facilitate the process effectively.
- Provisions for some honorarium should be thought of for the social audit committee members for conducting the audit. This will serve as a motivation for them to contribute to the process.
- It should be mandatory to mention on the Panchayat Bhawan wall that complaint register is available with the Panchayat for the public to lodge any complaint. Greater transparency will encourage

many workers to lodge complaints. During the field visit very less information was found written on the wall painting.

- Panchayats should be encouraged to prepare self disclosure document. Greater transparency will lead to move effective information sharing and reduced grievances.
- The vigilance and monitoring committees need to be strengthened. There were detailed instructions from the state on the structure and roles of the vigilance and monitoring committees. Adequate capacity building of the committees must be ensured so that they are able to monitor the ongoing works in MGNREGA.
- Local leaders (preferably those who have contested panchayat elections in the past), should be identified for strengthening the committees.
- Adequate role of Sarpanches should be thought out for ensuring transparency and accountability in the implementation of the scheme.

Investing in Improving Bank Payment System

Some households have reported that their wage payment is being realized in cash. A lot of this has to do with the inconveniences in accessing banking services by the workers. Banks are relatively away from the villages/ workers. Moreover, banks have operational difficulties in dealing with large number of small account holders who are illiterate and unfamiliar with formal banking system. In this regard, it is suggested that:

Despite old age Joseph relies on MGNREGA

Joseph Bhengra, Rainchapal, Kumjharia, Sundergarh

Joseph Bhengra is a 60 year old tribal belonging to Munda tribe, who lives in Beldipa hamlet of Kuarmunda village. Despite his old age he never loses a chance to work under MGNREGA. He is living in a joint family and has ownership over a small patch of land. As the earning from agriculture is not enough to sustain the family, Joseph along with his family members work as daily wage earners. Because there is no availability of job in their villages and nearby area, his two elder sons Robin and Kailash migrate out (seasonally) every year to add to the income of the family. Last year he had earned Rs.9000 from MGNREGA by working in a road construction work. Now he is not able to work due to his physical condition but he is happy with the income received from MGNREGS last year. From that income he could buy some agricultural appliances and he spent around four thousand for the family. This year (in January 2012) he has applied for land development support under MGNREGA, but he is yet to receive any confirmation. Since January 2012 his job card is kept in the Panchayat office.

- Workers need to be oriented on the procedure of banking so that they feel comfortable to visit bank by themselves and understand their entries. This will reduce the use of agents who mostly cheat the illiterate workers.
- There is a need to engage with the banks for the provision of ATM machines at a cluster of villages/ block headquarters. The workers thumb impression can be the basis of identification. Moreover, the ATM machines will also help reduce the difficulty of distances of the banks and fixed timings and fixed days for the payments of the MGNREGA wages.
- Since the banking infrastructure (branches as well as ATMs) are not available at the Panchayat level, other modes of wages payment through bank needs to be promoted. Bio-Metric cards can be an effective technology for disbursement of wages at the village level itself. The banks can appoint agents for carrying these ATMs to the village for wage distribution. There is also a need to explore the possibilities of paying the honorarium / salary of these agents through MGNREGA. This can become a potential area where the educated unemployed youth can be engaged.

Integrating MGNREGA Plans With Integrated District Planning

The level of engagement of the Gram Sabha is very low as far as planning for MGNREGA is concerned. Nevertheless plans are being prepared for the scheme in each panchayat. Inadequate planning leads to inability of the panchayats to take up more activities resulting in deficient response (in terms of number of days of work provided or delay in providing works) to the demand for work raised by the community. There is also a need to look at the plans from an integrated perspective where the works of MGNREGA can be converged with other line departments. As of now, convergence is driven only by the directives from the state government. There may be several opportunities for converging of different departments locally. In this regard the following may be considered:

- The MGNREGA should instruct all district level officials to derive the plan from the integrated plan document being prepared for the district.
- At the beginning of each year, plans thus derived should be painted on the walls of the panchayat so that people are aware of the works that will be done in the scheme with proposed months,

budget etc. This would also fall in line with the provision of self disclosure under RTI Act.

- Farmers belonging to SC/ST/BPLcategory who demands MGNREGA work on their land (as per the minimum requirement of sub scheme) should be provided the work in a guaranteed manner. This will increase the number of activities which can be taken up in the village and the panchayats will be able to respond adequately to the demand.
- Plans should essentially focus on converging with activities of some key departments that deal with agriculture, water resources, and rural development.
- Need to promote greater number of activities and convergence around strengthening agriculture. Most of the MGNREGA workers are directly or indirectly dependent on agriculture. Focusing on agriculture would help in making sustainable opportunities of livelihood for the workers.

Adding income of the family – thanks to farm pond under MGNREGA

Kalandi Mohanta, Baadsiadimal, Sunapantha, Harichandanpur, Keonjhar

Kalandi Mohanta, son of Jayakrushna, belongs to Kudumi (OBC) caste and is a resident of Badasiadimal village. He lives with his two brothers, one sister and old parents. Kalandi applied for a farm pond under MGNREGA during 2008 and got Rs.30,000 for the same. The Farm Pond was dug within 30 days engaging 15 villagers. Now the farm pond is being used for irrigating the land. Apart from paddy cultivation the family is growing vegetables and other crops with the help of the farm pond. Kalandi recounts that he got a profit of Rs.10, 000 from agriculture due to the farm pond. Now he is happy to announce that he is planning to go for fishery from next year.

Speeding up Measurement of Works

Delay in wage realization and lack of transparency in measurement results in drop of enthusiasm of people in working in MGNREGA. Often wages are deducted based on the measurement of work. Majority of the households who worked in MGNREGA stated that they received delayed wage payments. The poorest of the poor who work in MGNREGA cannot practically afford this delay. The absolute wage realisation is also lower than what is guaranteed by the Act. This results in the workers to look for other livelihood options available and also migrate in search of work. In this regard, the following suggestions may be considered:

- The huge gap of the services of engineers in the programme needs to be addressed by hiring them on an urgent basis. In case, hiring of sub engineers is not feasible quickly, the government should adopt measures for hiring local educated youth as barefoot engineers. Proper orientation of these youth should be undertaken and they should be given the task of measurement of simpler works like constructing farm bunds, ponds, roads. The sub engineers may be given the task of measuring more complicated tasks like well construction, large ponds, etc.
- Simple learning matter should be prepared by the state to identify with measurements. This can be used as a set instrument by the barefoot engineers, Panchayat representatives, vigilance and monitoring committee members and the social audit team members.

Chapter - VIII

The Road Ahead

Awareness should be created on the provisions, welfare facilities, wages rate, unemployment benefits, and accidental benefits among the villagers through audio-visual aids. Wall painting was found a good tool for awareness generation but maximum information should be given related to the provisions of MGNREGS besides 100 days of employment.

Due to lack of awareness people are not demanding for job under MGNREGS. If at all they are demanding they are dissuaded not to give the same in writing citing non availability of work and fund. It should be made mandatory to receive the job application by giving dated receipt to all the beneficiaries.

- The state should engage with a professional communication agency to redesign the communication strategy on a priority basis. Build awareness at block and village levels among beneficiaries, local officials, teachers, village elders, panchayat members, and media persons. Form awareness-committees consisting of educated youth. Train panchayat representatives in planning.
- Hold camps to enable the potential beneficiaries to question the lacunae related to entitlements and rights.
- Communicate details regarding projects sanctioned and the amount sanctioned through display boards.
- The state should issue instructions at the district level to identify and engage civil society organisations for awareness generation.
- There is a need to initiate discussion with the concerned officials on including MGNREGA in Service Guarantee Act. This process

should begin with the distribution of basic entitlements like job cards, recording of verbal applications, opening of bank accounts, etc. may be included.

- Panel of retired civil engineers should be identified and be engaged for measurement of works.

The target population expressed that MGNREGS should continue with some improvement in the implementation process so that maximum benefits could be received by the targeted beneficiaries.

- Gram Sabha meeting should be organised regularly and the local villagers should be a part of identification and prioritization of work and also the decision making process under the MGNREGS. Transparency should be maintained during preparing muster rolls and during payment.
- There is need to enhance peoples participation in decision making process during selection of work under MGNREGS.
- Women participation should be increased and ensure allotment of work to at least one-third of the women who ask for it.
- Ensure provision of crèches at worksites and all facilities should be provided to them at workplace as mentioned in the MGNREGA so that MGNREGS objectives could be achieved with the development of target population.
- Ensure gender parity in payment of wages.
- Gram Rozgar Sewak should be provided proper training and information as per their role and responsibilities related to MGNREGS.
- The Gram Rozgar Sewak is given the responsibility to update the Job Card, this need to be reiterated and enforced.
- There should be no tolerance towards handling and hoarding of Job Cards by other - implementing officials, PRI members and contractors.
- Welfare related facility should be make available at work site.
- More focus should be given for development of agriculture related assets at household as well as community level.
- The job cards and the pass books should remain with labourer and wage payment should be on time.

MGNREGS should be implemented as per law. It is suggested that there should be a separate department dealing with MGNREGS to ensure timely payment of wages and transparency. There should be more officials dealing with such issues.

Ensure that the implementing agency gives a dated receipt to the applicants in order to enable them to claim unemployment allowance. Unemployment allowance need to be implemented in case beneficiaries did not get work after application.

- Capacity of PRI members should be enhanced so that they could effectively monitor the MGNREGS projects in their respective areas.
- The Programme Officer and the District Programme Coordinators should be made accountable for monitoring of the projects carried out in their respective areas.
- Private engineers and architects may be engaged to do the basic measurement and filling of formats for measurement which can then be verified by the appointed civil engineer. This will relieve the load on the existing technical staff.
- Intensive capacity building should be organised for the Panchayat representatives and Secretaries on preparation of labour budget.
- During the Gram Sabha Meeting approved budget should be shared with the villagers.
- Provisions should be made for making payment to the Social Audit Committee members for conducting Social Audits. The payment can be a part of the work budget so that it can be booked as wages to workers.
- The Social Audit Committee should be strengthened by including non workers and mentors in the committee.
- Social audit should be done every year.
- The state should conduct a study on the effectiveness of convergence approach in MGNREGA. The study should highlight the challenges emerging in the approach and how to make convergence work for the state.
- A state level high powered committee should be set-up to supervise the convergence of various schemes. The committee should organise regular meetings to push forward the convergence of various departments with MGNREGA.
- The state should review the wage rates for different works undertaken in the scheme.

- Grievance registers to be made mandatory in all GPs and blocks. Special responsibility should be given to implementing officials at GP and block level to keep the record at their level.

As has been perceived under MGNREGS Social Audit should be organised with the aim to ensure transparency, ensure public accountability, ensure participation of community, ensure consent and consultation and ensure grievance redressal mechanism. This has been proven that social audit could also be an effective tool for awareness generation. With these objectives social audit should be organized in all the states.

The MGNREGA programme, reorganized on these lines, holds out the prospect of not only transforming livelihoods of the poorest people of our country but also be harbinger towards a revolution in rural governance in India.

Bibliography

Afridi, F., Sharan, M. & Iversen, V. (2012). 'Does female leadership impact on governance? Evidence from a public poverty alleviation programme in Andhra Pradesh, India'. Mimeo.

Allaoua, Z et al. (1997). India: Achievment and challenges in reducing Poverty, Washington, D.C: The World Bank.

Ambasta, P., Vijay Shankar, P.S., Shah, M. (2008), Two years of NREGA: The Road ahead, *Economic & Political Weekly*, Vol. 43, No. 8, pp. 41-50.

Arulampalam, W., Dasgupta, S., Dhillon, A. & Dutta, B. (2009). 'Electoral goals and centre-state transfers: A theoretical model and empirical evidence from India', *Journal of Development Economics*, Vol. 88, No. 1, pp. 103-119.

Arvind Singh Bisht, (19 February 2006). Rural employment: No guarantee yet, Times of India, Retrieved from https://timesofindia.indiatimes.com on 09/02/2018.

Axine, Olson. (20 October 2005), Work for pro-poor growth, The Economic Times.

Azam, M. (2011). The impact of Indian job guarantee scheme on labor market outcomes: Evidence from a natural experiment (Unpublished manuscript).

Banerjee, A. & Somanathan, R. (2007). 'The political economy of public goods: Some evidence from India', *Journal of Development Economics,* Vol. 82, No. 2, pp. 287-314.

Banerjee, A. and Somanathan, R. (2007). 'The political economy of public goods: Some evidence from India'. *Journal of Development Economics*, Vol. 82, No. 2, pp. 287-314.

Bardhan, P. & Mookherjee, D. (2000). 'Capture and governance at local and national levels'. *The American Economic Review*, Vol. 90, No. 2., pp. 135-139.

Bardhan, P. & Mookherjee, D. (2000). 'Capture and governance at local and national levels'. *The American Economic Review*, Vol. 90, No. (2), pp. 135-139.

Bardhan, P. & Mookherjee, D. (2010), "Determinants of redistribution politics: An empirical analysis of land reforms in West Bengal, India'. *The American Economic Review,* Vol. 100, No. 4, pp. 1572-1600.

Bardhan, P. & Mookherjee, D. (2010), "Determinants of redistribution politics: An empirical analysis of land reforms in West Bengal, India'. *The American Economic Review*, Vol. 100, No. 4, pp. 1572-1600.

Barrett, C. B. & Clay, D. C.(2003). "Self-targeting accuracy in the presence of imperfect factor markets: Evidence from food-for-work in ethiopia". *Journal of Development Studies*, Vol. 39, No. 5, pp. 152–180.

Bassi, N., Kumar, D. M., Niranjan, V., & Sivamohan, M. (2011). 'Employment guarantee and its environmental impact: Are the claims valid?'. *Economic and Political Weekly,* Vol. 46, No. 34.

Besley, T., Pande, R. & Rao, V. (2005). 'Political selection and the quality of government: Evidence from South India'. Yale Economic growth Discussion Paper No 921.

Besley, T. & Coate, S., (1997). 'An economic model of representative democracy', *Quarterly Journal of Economics,* Vol. 112, No. 2, pp. 85-114.

Besley, T. & Coate, S. (2003). 'Centralized versus decentralized provision of local public goods: A political economy approach'. *Journal of Public Economics,* Vol.87, No. 2, pp. 2611 – 2637.

Besley, T., Pande, R., Rahman, R. & Rao, V. (2004). 'The politics of public good provision: Evidence from Indian local governments'. Journal of European Economic Association, 2(3), 416–426.

Bhatia, B. and J. Drèze. (2006). "Employment guarantee in Jharkand: Ground realities." *Economic and Political Weekly*, Vol. 41, No.29, pp. 3198–3202.

Census of India, 2001 & 2011,

Centre for Budget and Governance Accountability. (15 September 2007), Report on emplementation of NREGA, in Andhra Pradesh, Chhattisgarh, Jharkhand, and Madhya Pradesh in May and June 2006,

Chakraborty, P. (2007). Implementation of employment Guarantee: A preliminary appraisal, *Economic & Political Weekly*, Vol. 42, No. 7, pp. 548-551.

Chakraborty, P. (2007). 'Implementation of employment guarantee: A preliminary appraisal'. Economic and Political Weekly, Vol. 42, No.7,pp. 548-551.

Chattopadhyay, R. & Duflo, E. (2004). 'Women as policy makers: Evidence from a randomized policy experiment in India'. *Econometrica*, Vol.72, No. 5, pp. 1409-1443.

Cherian, Thomas. (14 September 2005) Adding jobs, but at what cost?. International Herald Tribune. Chhabra, S., Raina, R. L. & Sharma, G.L., (2010). MGNREGA: A step towards meeting the challenges of inclusive growth: A study of six states, LBS Journal of Management & Research, Vol. 8, No.1, pp 123-149.

Chhibber, P.&Nooruddin, I. (2004). 'Do party systems count', Comparative Political Studies, Vol. 37, No.2, pp. 152-87.

Chopra, D. (2011a). 'Interaction of 'power' in the making and shaping of social policy'. Contemporary South Asia, Vol. 19, No. 2, pp. 153-171.

Chopra, D. (2011b). 'Policy making in India: A dynamic process of statecraft'. Pacific Affairs, Vol. 84, No. 1,pp. 89-107.

Coady, D., M. Grosh, & J. Hoddinott. 2004. "Targeting Outcomes Redux." World Bank Research Observer, Vol.19, No. 1, pp.61–85.

Comptroller and Auditor General Report. (31 March 2009). Retrieved from http://ezinearticles.com/?Labour-Migration:-A-Shadow-of-Poverty-in-Orissa&id=115270 on 31.01.2013.

Dalapati, T. K. (2010). MGNREGS in Madhya Pradesh: Loopholes, silver linings and ways ahead, *LBS Journal of Management & Research,* Vol. 8, No.1, pp. 72-84.

De Neve, G. & Carswell, G. (2011). 'NREGA and the return of identity politics in Western Tamil Nadu, India'. *Forum for Development Studies,* Vol. 38, No. 2, pp. 205-210.

Devi, Pajula, A.K.(1986). "Poverty in rural areas: A study", *Kurukshetra,* Vol. XXXV, No. 2-3,

Dre'ze, Jean & Siddhartha, Lal, (13 July, 2007), The Hindu,

Dreze J & R. Khera (2011), In: Reetika, Khera (Ed.). (2011). The battle for employment guarantee, pp. 43–81, New Delhi: Oxford University Press.Dreze, Jean, Khera, Reetika, Siddarth, NREGA in Orissa*: Ten Loopholes and the Silver Lining*" Interim Survey report

Dreze, J. & Khera, R. (2010). 'The BPL census and a possible alternative'. *Economic and Political Weekly*, Vol. 45, No. 9, pp. 54-63.

Dutta, R., Murgai, R., Ravallion, M., & van de Walle, D.,(2012). "Does India's employment guarantee scheme guarantee employment?". *Economic and Political Weekly*, Vol. 47,No.16, pp. 55–64.

FAO (2016b). Addressing rural youth migration at its root causes: A conceptual framework. Rome: FAO.

http://www.fao.org/3/a-i5718e.pdf

Gaiha, R., Kulkarni, V. S., Pandey, M. K. & Imai, K.S. (2010). National Rural Employment Guarantee Scheme, Poverty and prices in rural India. *Journal of Asian and African Studies*, Vol. 45, No. 6, pp. 645-669.

Gangadharan, T.P. & Jalma Rao, V. (1998).Employment generation in non-farm sector: NABARD's Role, op.cit., 1998.

Ghose, Arabindo.(16-31 December 1986). "On Reducing Poverty Speedily". *Yojana*.Government of India. (2012). MGNREGA SAMEEKSHA MoRD.

Government of India. (2012). Operational Guidelines 2008, MoRD, GoI

Government of Odisha, Annual Report, 2006-07 of Department of Panchayati Raj.

Government of Odisha, Annual Report, 2007-08 of Department of Panchayati Raj.

Guidelines on Convergence With National Rural Employment Guarantee Scheme, Department of Rural Development Ministry of Rural Development Government of India.

Gupta, M.S. (2009). Rural labour: Problems and prospects: Serial publication.

Hirway, Indira (April 1988). "Planning for poverty eradication in rural areas: An observation", *Kurukshetra*, Vol. XXXVI, pp 17.

Imbert, C. & J. Papp. 2012, "Equilibrium distributional impacts of Government employment programs: Evidence from India's employment guarantee", *Paris School of Economics,* Working Paper retrieved from .

Indian Institute of Technology, Appraisal of Processes and Procedures of NREGS in Orissa: A study of Mayurbhanj and Balasore District: Department of Humanities and Social Sciences, Kharagpur (Submitted to Ministry of Rural Development, Government of India).

Indira Hirway, M.R.Saluja and Bhupesh Yadav, 'Assessing Multiplier impact of NREGA Works through Village SAM Modelling' Retrieved from http://www.economistsforfullemployment.org/news/documents/Hirway_nana_kotda_SAM.pdf

International Labour Organization (ILO), (2010). 'MGNREGA: A Review of Recent Work and Green Jobs in Kaimur District in Bihar', Geneva: ILO.

Jandu, Navjyoti. (16-17 September 2008). "Employment Guarantee and Women's Empowerment in Rural India", paper presented to International Seminar on National Rural Employment Guarantee Scheme in India, organized by Institute for Human Development and Centre de Science Humaines, held at New Delhi.

Jeetsingh, Sanwal. (2012). *Rozgar ke intezar mein Rozgar Guarunty Ka Mazboor, Hashiye Ki Awaz,* September 2012, p. 20.

Jha, Raghbendra., Gaiha, Raghav., & Shankar, Shylashri., (2008). Economic & Political Weekly, March 15.

Jha, R. & Gaiha, R. (2012). NREGS: Interpreting the official statistics, *Eco*nomic & Political Weekly, Vol. 47, No. 40, pp. 18-22.

Judge, Paramjit Singh. (1989). "Scheduled Castes and Development from Above". In: (ed. P.N. Pimply, K.P. Singh & A., Mahajan, Social Development Process & Consequences. Jaipur: Rawat Publications.

Karunakaran, C. (1998). From the Compilation Fifty Years of Rural Development in India: Retrospect and Prospect, p. 41.

Khemani, S. (2004). 'Political cycles in a developing economy: Effect of elections in the Indian States'. *Journal of Development Economics*, Vol. 73, No. 1, pp. 125-154.

Khera, R. (13 July 2006). Employment Guarantee and Migration. The Hindu.

———————— (2008) Implementation of Employment Guarantee: A Preliminary Appraisal, *Economic & Political Weekly*, Vol. 43, No. 35, pp. 8-10.

Khera, R. & Nayak, N. (2008). Women workers and perceptions of the National Rural Employment Guarantee Act.*Economic & Political Weekly*, Vol. 44, No. 43, pp. 49-57.

Khera, Reetika (Ed.), 2011. The battle for employment guarantee. Oxford: Oxford University Press.

Khosla, R. (2011). 'Caste, politics and public goods distribution in India: Evidence from NREGS in Andhra Pradesh'. *Economic and Political Weekly,* Vol. 46, No.12, pp. 63-69.

Kulkarni, G., Batta, Rama Chandra & Ganesh Kumar,N. (1989). "Integrated Rural Development in Bijapur: An Evaluation of Dairy Scheme". *Social Change*, Vol. 19, No. 89, pp. 78.

Kumar, A. A., (2010.) 'Effectiveness and Ownership of Irrigation Assets Created under MGNREGA and Labour Market Dynamics in Bihar'.Anand: Institute of Rural Management,

Louis, P. (2006). 'NREGS Implementation II: Birth Pangs in Bihar'. Vol. 41, No. 48, pp. 4946-4947.

MacAuslan, I. (2008). 'India: National Rural Employment Guarantee Act: A case study for how change happens' in Green, D. (ed.) From poverty to power: How active citizens and effective states can change the world. Oxfam International Press.

Mahapatra Devi Prasad: A shadow of Poverty in Orissa; *Orissa diary, 2005*

Mathur, L. (2007) Employment Guarantee: Progress so Far, *Economic & Political Weekly*, Vol. 42, No. 52, (December 29), pp. 17-20.

Mehrotra, S. (2008) NREG Two Years on: Where Do We Go from Here?, *Economic & Political Weekly*, Vol. 43, No. 31 , (August 2), pp. 27-35.

Meshwari, S.R. (1985). Rural Development in India: A Public Policy Approach, Sage Publications, New Delhi Ch 22, pp 217.

Mishra, P., Behera, B. and Nayak, N.C. (2010) A Development Delivery Institution for the Tribal Communities: Experience of the National Rural Employment Guarantee Scheme in India, *Development Policy Review*, Vol. 28, No. 4, 457-479.

Misra, S.N and M Behera (2000), *A comparative study of Nutritional Support to Primary Education (Mid-day meals Scheme) in Orissa and Tamil Nadu*, Nabakrushna Choudhury Centre for Development Studies, Bhubaneswar

Mohammad Iqbal, Public vigilance helps to minimise corruption in rural employment guarantee scheme, The Hindu, 28 April, 2006

National Sample Survey, (2010) Round 66. National Sample Survey. Office, Ministry of Statistics and Programme Implementation of the Government of India. http://164.100.34.58/index.php/catalog/18.

Niehaus, P. and S. Sukhtankar. 2011. "Corruption Dynamics: The Golden Goose Effect." Unpublished Manuscript, University of California, San Diego. http://dss.ucsd.edu/~pniehaus/papers/nrega.pdf.

Niehaus, P. and Sukhtankar, S. (2011). 'The Marginal rate of corruption in public programmes'. [Online resource available at: http://dss.ucsd.edu/ ~ pniehaus/papers/leakage.pdf Accessed on 20th August 2012.

Panda, R.K, and Asima Sahu: Trends and Dimensions of Rural Poverty in Orissa; *Orissa overview*, September- October, 2011

Pande, R. (2003). 'Can mandated political representation increase policy influence for disadvantaged minorities? Theory and evidence from India'. American Economic Review 93 (4), 1132-1151.

Pankaj, A. K., and A. N. Sharma, (2008.)Understanding the Processes, Institutions and Mechanisms of Implementation and Impact Assessment of NREGA in Bihar and Jharkhand , New Delhi: Institute of Human Development (IHD),

Planning And Implementation of National Rural Employment Guarantee Scheme In Madhya Pradesh (A Process Study), Institute of Rural Development, Rajendra Nagar,Hyderabad,April-2010

Pradeep Baisakh "MGNREGA performs poorly in poverty stricken Odisha" http://infochangeindia.org/poverty/features/mgnrega-performs-poorly-in-poverty-stricken-orissa.html visited 3.2.2013

Rajlaxmi Kamath, Rajluxmi Murthy and Trilochan Sastry, 'NREGA Surveys in Ananatpur, Adilabad, Raichur and Gulbarga' www.nrega.net/pin/reports-and...to.../NREGA%20IIMB.doc

Ramanujam, M.S., I.C. Awasthi and Gayatri Pande (1998). Rural Employment: Past, Present and Future, op.cit., 1998, pp 40.

Rao, Sudhakar B. (1998). Poverty, Employment and Growth: An Overview, in Fifty Years of Rural Development in India: Retrospect and Prospect, New Delhi. (Rath, from the compilation Fifty Years of Rural Development in India: Retrospect and Prospect, 1998, pp 44).

Reetika Khera and Nandini Nayak (2009).Women Workers and Perceptions of the National Rural Employment Guarantee Act. Economic & Political Weekly EPW OCTOBER 24, vol xliv no 43.

Sabharwal, M. & Reddy, K. (2009). Making India's labour markets inclusive, *Review of Market Integration*, Vol. 1, No. 3, pp. 265-293.

Samaj Pragati Sahayog, & Megh Pyne Abhiyan, (2011). Leveraging MGNREGA for Flood Control in Bihar: A Case for Policy Reform in Bihar,

Sankaran, K. (2011). 'NREGA wages: Ensuring decent work'. *Economic and Political Weekly,* Vol. 46, No. 7, pp. 23-25.

Saxena, N., Gaiha, R., Kurian, N., Sainath, P., Mander, H., Seddey, S., Roy, M., Raju, K., Singh, M., Sandhu, G., Misra, A., Singh, A., Kumar, A., Lakka, W., Roy, A., Gautam, S. & Datta, K. (2009). Report of the expert group on the methodology for BPL census. New Delhi: Ministry of Rural Development.Retrieved from http://rural.nic.in/ Reportof Expert Group Chaired- Dr.N.C.Saxena.pdfon 14th August 2012.

Sebastian Morris. (30 August 2005)Employment Guarantee Scheme is a still-born child: Try land reforms, Financial Express.

Sen, Amartya. (2001), Development as freedom, New Delhi: Oxford University Press.

Shah T, S. Verma, R. Indu & P. Hemant, (2010). Asset Creation through Employment Guarantee? Synthesis of Student Case Studies in Nine States of India. New Delhi: International Water Management Institute (IWMI).

Shah, Mihir. (2004). 'National Rural Employment Guarantee Act: A Historic Opportunity', The Economic and Political Weekly, December, 11.Shankar, S. & Gaiha, R. (2011), 'Networks and anti-Poverty programmes: The NREGS experience", ASARC Working Paper 2011/ 05.

Sharma, P.N. (1988). "IRDP and Poverty Alleviation Strategies: An Appraisal", Kurukshetra, Vol. XXXVI, No. 6, p 18.

Sharma, S.K. & Malhotra, S.L. (1977). Integrated Rural Development: Approach, Strategies and Perspectives. New Delhi: Abhinav Publications.

Shekhar, Chander. (21 May 1987). "Evaluation of IRDP", The Tribune. p. 4.

Siddhartha, A.V. (2008). CAG report on NREGA: Fact and fiction, *Economic & Political Weekly*, Vol. 43, No. 25, pp. 39-45.

Singh VS. (1-15 April1988). "An insight into Poverty Alleviation Programmes". *Yojana*, Vol.32, No.6, p. 8.

Singh, Jasbir K. (1988). "Socio-Economic Impact of Integrated Rural Development Programme on Weaker Section in Punjab". *Guru Nanak Journal of Sociology*, Vol. 9, No. 1.

Singh, V.S. & Lal, Banwari (1987). "Poverty Analysis – Where does it Lead", *Man and Development*, Vol. IX, No. 3,

Sinha, R. K., & Marandi, R. K. (2011). 'Impact of NREGA on wage rates food secuirty and rural urban migration in Bihar', Report submitted to the Ministry of Agriculture, Bhagalpur: Agro-economic Research Centre for Bihar and Jharkhand.

Sinha, Sanjay. (1986). "Poverty Alleviation: Anything Goes", *Economic and Political Weekly,* Vol. 24 , No. 19, Volume 24, pp. 823.

Sivakumar, S. (2010). 'A political agenda to minimise wages." *Economic and Political Weekly*, Vol. 45, No. 50, pp.10-12.

Sjoblom, D, & J. Farrington. (2008). "The Indian National Rural Employment Guarantee Act: Will it reduce poverty and boost the economy?", Overseas Development Institute Project Briefing No. 7. London: Overseas Development Institute. Retrieved from www.odi.org.uk/resources/docs/614.pdf.

Sonu, Jain, (3 February 2006). Job guarantee rolls out, ray of hope in New Delhi shadow, The Indian Express.

Sridhar, V. 2005.'Empowering the rural poor', Frontline, Vol. 22, Issue 19, Sep 10-23

Srikanth, Goparaju & Shome, Samik. (January-June 2011). What need for MGNREA? *IIMS-Journal of Management Science*, Vol.2, pp.54-60.

Srivastava, D.K., Sanyal S.K., Bhujanga Rao C., & Chakraborty, P. (2007). Rural poverty in Madhya Pradesh: Looking beyond conventional measures, *Economic & Political Weekly*, Vol. 42, No. 5, pp. 381-388.

Status Report on Convergence Initiatives of MGNRGA in India. (April 2010) National Institute of Rural Development, Hyderabad.

Swamy, R., ((2010) 'The Mahatma Gandhi National Rural Employment Guarantee Act: A study of Andhra Pradesh and Bihar'. (Masters Dissertation, Department of Social Policy London School of Economics and Political Science)..

Tenaja, Suresh (9 February 1989). "Long Search for Savers", The Tribune. p 6.

The Gazette of India, Extra-ordinary Part II-Section I, Ministry of Law and Justice, India. retrieved from http://nrega.nic.in/rajaswa.pdf accessed on 29th August 2011.

The National Rural Employment Guarantee Act. (2005). (NREGA), Ministry of Rural Development Government of India, New Delhi.

Vaidyanathan, A. (2001). 'Poverty and Development Policy', *Economic and Political Weekly*, Vol XXXVI, No 21-Venkat R. Chary. (9 September 2005).NREGS: Grossly miscalculated? The Hindu Business Line.

Verma, S., (2011). 'Multiple Use Water Services in India: Scaling up Community-based MUS through MGNREGA', International Water Management Institute (IWMI),Sri Lanka.

Verma, S., (2011).'MGNREGA assets and rural water security: Synthesis of field studies in Bihar, Gujarat, Kerala and Rajasthan', Anand: International Water Management Institute.

Yunus, Muhammad, (1997). Towards creating a poverty-free world, New Delhi: Institute of Social Sciences.

Zaman, H. (2011). Assessing the impact of employment generation programs in challenging rural poverty: A comparative study on Bangladesh and India. *Journal on Poverty*, Vol. 15, No. 3, pp. 259-276.

Index

X